LEADING
With **DATA**

Leadership for Learning

Series Editors
Willis D. Hawley and E. Joseph Schneider

Joseph Murphy
Leadership for Literacy: Research-Based Practice, PreK–3

P. Karen Murphy, Patricia A. Alexander
Understanding How Students Learn: A Guide for Instructional Leaders

E. Joseph Schneider, Lara L. Hollenczer
The Principal's Guide to Managing Communication

Kenneth A. Strike
Ethical Leadership in Schools: Creating Community in an Environment of Accountability

Karen Hawley Miles, Stephen Frank
The Strategic School: Making the Most of People, Time, and Money

Sharon D. Kruse, Karen Seashore Louis
Building Strong School Cultures: A Guide to Leading Change

Ellen Goldring, Mark Berends
Leading With Data: Pathways to Improve Your School

Please call our toll-free number (800-818-7243)
or visit our Web site (www.corwinpress.com)
to order individual titles or the entire series.

LEADING
With
DATA

Pathways to
Improve Your School

Ellen Goldring • Mark Berends

For information:

Corwin Press
A SAGE Company
2455 Teller Road
Thousand Oaks, California 91320
www.corwinpress.com

SAGE India Pvt. Ltd.
B 1/I 1 Mohan Cooperative
  Industrial Area
Mathura Road, New Delhi 110 044
India

SAGE Ltd.
1 Oliver's Yard
55 City Road
London, EC1Y 1SP
United Kingdom

SAGE Asia-Pacific Pte. Ltd.
33 Pekin Street #02–01
Far East Square
Singapore 048763

Printed in the United States of America.

Library of Congress Cataloging-in-Publication Data

Goldring, Ellen B. (Ellen Borish), 1957-
 Leading with data : pathways to improve your school / Ellen Goldring,
Mark Berends.
     p. cm.—(Leadership for learning series)
 "A joint publication with the American Association of School Administrators."
 Includes bibliographical references and index.
 ISBN 978-0-7619-8833-5 (cloth)—ISBN 978-0-7619-8834-2 (pbk.)
 1. School management and organization—Data processing. 2. School management and organization—Decision making. 3. School improvement programs. I. Berends, Mark, 1962– II. American Association of School Administrators. III. Title. IV. Series.

LB2806.17.G65 2009
371.2—dc22

2008022886

This book is printed on acid-free paper.

08 09 10 11 12   10 9 8 7 6 5 4 3 2 1

Acquisitions Editor: Arnis Burvikovs
Editorial Assistant: Irina Dragut
Associate Editor: Desirée A. Bartlett
Production Editor: Appingo Publishing Services
Cover Designer: Lisa Miller
Graphic Designer: Scott Van Atta

Contents

Acknowledgments

Leadership is complex. High-quality leadership for school improvement is even more complex. We have learned about the power of leading with data as a path toward focusing leadership on student learning from a group of talented school principals and insightful colleagues. Our journey started with the Principal's Leadership Academy of Nashville (PLAN). We have had the extraordinary opportunity to develop and refine our ideas about data and leadership throughout our work with school leaders in PLAN. We have been extremely fortunate to have ongoing and valuable feedback. We acknowledge this support from the principals and teachers of PLAN.

Dr. Pearl Sims, founding director of PLAN, has contributed greatly to our understanding of the art of strategic planning, and Dr. Steve Baum, Dr. Marcy Singer-Gabella, and Tom Ward have kept us grounded in the reality of the work of school leadership. We thank the other design team principals—Darwin Mason, Laura Hall, Lori Donahue, Paul Flemming, Robert Sasser, and Susan Burns—who have helped guide the development of the ideas presented in this book. We also thank Dr. Paul Changes, director of research and evaluation from the Metropolitan Nashville Public Schools, who provided access to data and his own experience in using data for school improvement.

At Vanderbilt we have benefited from graduate students and colleagues giving of their time and expertise: Anna Nicotera, Xiu Cravens, and Patrick Schuermann all provided ongoing support and insights that greatly improved upon our ideas and enhanced the overall quality of our work. We are indebted to Dr. Bill Hawley, who invited us to write this book. He provided us with timely and pointed feedback as he read earlier drafts of the manuscript and kept us engaged with this project to ensure its completion when competing demands kept emerging. We thank the wonderful practitioners and our colleagues for sharing with us their experiences and perspectives about leading with data.

PUBLISHER'S ACKNOWLEDGMENTS

Corwin Press would like to acknowledge the following reviewers:

Margarete Couture
Principal
South Seneca Central School District
Interlaken, NY

Jo Lane Hall
Principal
Center for Knowledge, Richland School District Two
Columbia, SC

Kathryn Harwell Kee
PCC, Leadership Coach and Consultant
Coaching School Results
Shady Shores, TX

Gary E. Martin
Professor
Northern Arizona University
Flagstaff, AZ

Helane Smith Miller
Assistant Principal
DC Public Schools
Washington, DC

Cathy Patterson
Elementary Learning Specialist
Walnut Valley Unified School District
Diamond Bar, CA

About the Authors

Ellen Goldring (PhD, University of Chicago) is Professor of Education Policy and Leadership at Peabody College of Vanderbilt University. At Vanderbilt she won the Alexander Heard Distinguished Professor award. Her areas of expertise and research focus on improving schools with particular attention to educational leadership and access and equity in schools of choice. She is the immediate past coeditor of *Educational Evaluation and Policy Analysis*. She serves on numerous editorial boards, technical panels, and policy forums and is the coauthor of three books and hundreds of book chapters and articles, including the book *Principals of Dynamic Schools* (Corwin Press). She is a currently working on a project, funded by the Wallace Foundation, to develop and field-test an education leadership assessment system and establish its psychometric properties. She is also conducting experiments to study professional development and performance feedback for school leaders. She is an investigator at the National Center on School Choice and the Learning Sciences Institute at Vanderbilt.

Mark Berends (PhD Sociology, University of Wisconsin-Madison) is professor of sociology at the University of Notre Dame; director of the Center for Research on Educational Opportunity; director of the National Center on School Choice, funded by the U.S. Department of Education's Institute of Education Sciences (http://www.vanderbilt.edu/schoolchoice/); and the Vice President of the American Educational Research Association's Division L, Policy and Politics in Education. His areas of expertise are the sociology of education, research methods, school effects on student achievement, and educational equity. Throughout his research career, Professor Berends has focused on how school organization and classroom instruction are related to student achievement, with special attention to disadvantaged students. Within this agenda, he has applied a variety of quantitative and qualitative methods to understanding the effect of school reforms on teachers and students. His latest books are *Examining Gaps in Mathematics Achievement Among Racial-Ethnic Groups, 1972–1992* (2005), *Charter School Outcomes* (2008), and the *Handbook of Research on School Choice* (in press).

Foreword

This book, by Ellen Goldring and Mark Berends, deals with the practical, day-to-day aspects of data collection and analysis. As one principal who reviewed the book said, "This is a wonderful and comprehensive resource that is very practical and easy to understand." It is full of examples, cases, vignettes, and useful advice, but it does not burden the reader with minutia. And yet the book is much more than a how-to-do-it manual.

The two professors nest the use of data, broadly defined, in research on leadership and school improvement. They demonstrate how school leaders can use evidence of many kinds to develop the kind of practices and cultures that produce increased student learning.

Much of the interest in data utilization in schools has understandably focused on how best to use student-achievement data to meet the challenges of high-stakes accountability. Goldring and Berends take a broader and more proactive stance. They believe that although the collection and analysis of achievement data are critically important, understanding student performance also requires the use of other measures of student learning. And they recognize that knowing the extent to which students of different backgrounds and needs meet achievement goals is only the first step in the school-improvement process. Understanding why some students outperform others is also essential to data-based decision making. That understanding comes only from collecting, analyzing, and using data from many sources, including families and students themselves.

Data-based decision making is not just for school leaders and improvement teams. Nor is it just a beginning- and end-of-the-year activity. Goldring and Berends make a persuasive case for continuous collection and extensive use of evidence by the entire school community for both individual students and the school as a whole.

The authors add their voices to a growing chorus of scholars who advocate the wisdom of using data-based decision making for student achievement. Scarcely anybody argues against the approach. Schools in which student-centered collaborative problem solving is a way of life outperform others over and over again. But if it were easy, there would be many more schools in which evidence-based decision making was ubiquitous.

As Goldring and Berends illustrate, the use of data as a pathway to improvement is not just a technical process. The continuous examination of individual and school performance constantly calls into question whether there are more or better things to do to facilitate student learning. The constant use of data creates *disequilibrium,* and the attendant tensions can result in positive outcomes. Or it can create discouragement, which may lead individuals or the school community to retreat to more comfortable and less changeful postures. The outcome depends on the ways (there is not just one) leaders develop and sustain a culture of shared responsibility and ensure that teachers, staff, and students have the resources and support they need to sustain change based on their data analysis.

This book is one of a series edited as part of the Leadership for Learning initiative of the American Association of School Administrators. The primary purpose of the series is to provide school-level leaders with support in developing and sustaining a schoolwide capacity for continuous improvement. This book achieves that goal exceedingly well.

—Willis D. Hawley and E. Joseph Schneider

Section I

Improving Schools With Data

The Importance
of Data-Based
Decision Making

This chapter provides a general introduction to data-based decision making by addressing the question, why is using data for decision making important for school improvement? Today's effective educational leaders use data extensively to guide them in decision making, setting and prioritizing goals, and monitoring progress. They use data to define needs, set goals, plan interventions, and evaluate progress. The continuing analysis of the gaps between goals for student learning and student performance defines the actions of effective schools. Capable data-based decision makers understand the array of data that is needed for school improvement. They know some fundamental principles of measurement and assessment and can implement data-analysis skills. They use a multitude of strategies to analyze data to propel teaching and learning and school improvement. They use technology to support the use of data. They engage the school community (teachers, parents, students) in using data to analyze strengths, weakness, threats, and opportunities for school improvement. At the end of this chapter, you should be able to explain why data-driven decision making is critical for schools to meet the needs of all children and to reach accountability expectations.

VIGNETTE

Imagine you are a new principal with little previous administrative and leadership experience. You have taken your first job as a principal of Rosemont School. Rosemont serves students from kindergarten through Grade 8. As you begin this new role and establish new relationships with your staff, you face many demands. The greatest demand for you is guiding your school in a high-stakes accountability environment. Although your school has a highly qualified staff and supportive parents, your school must help students learn more and should, therefore, produce better results, particularly on the state-mandated assessments. When you were hired, you were informed by the district superintendent that Rosemont's test scores have declined during the past few years. You need a plan. A systematic one. One that will provide leadership to your school and maintain the support and morale of your staff and parents. What will you do? The first thing you know you must do is come to grips with understanding all the data available about your school, your staff, and your students. You desire to know how these data support Rosemont's vision and mission and how the data provide information for improving what occurs in your school.

As this vignette suggests, effective educational leaders can use data extensively to guide them in decision making. A primary goal of instructional leaders is to focus the staff on the mission and vision of the school. They also use the array of available data to inform the school community about how well they are progressing toward meeting the goals and objectives of that mission. Continuous improvement hinges on continuous data-based decision making.

Throughout this book we refer to Rosemont School to provide examples of data-based decision making in action. However, the examples are applicable to all schools. Rosemont School serves students in elementary and middle school grades. The guiding principles can also be applied to high schools. High schools are often much more complex than elementary and middle schools; however, the importance of data-based decision making is the same. The processes and the types and sources of data are similar. This book is for school leaders at all types of schools.

Why is data-driven decision making so crucial for school improvement? Why are leaders turning to data to help drive their leadership? In this chapter we present the major reasons for engaging in data-driven decision making and provide an overview of the literature and theory supporting data-driven decision making in schools. After first discussing the role of data-based decision making within the context of a standards-based reform framework, we then discuss four key reasons for data-driven decision making:

- To work toward continuous improvement
- To meet accountability requirements

- To focus efforts and monitor progress
- To develop a sense of community through organizational learning

STANDARDS-BASED REFORM AND DATA-BASED DECISION MAKING

Since 1969, the Gallup organization has conducted systematic annual surveys of public opinion on a number of issues regarding public education. From the resulting reams of data have come various trends, both nationally and internationally, that suggest that too many students in the United States are not proficient in mathematics and reading and that the United States lags behind many of our international competitors. Multiple waves of these national and international studies over the past couple of decades suggest that the U.S. educational system is not progressing to meet our expectations and desires. In fact, some are quite skeptical that U.S. schools are making steady progress in educating students, pointing to indicators from a battery of national and international standardized tests such as the National Assessment of Educational Progress (NAEP), the International Assessment of Educational Progress (IAEP), and the International Evaluation of Achievement (IEA). Critics cite seemingly mediocre or poor test scores as evidence that American public schools are failing in their missions to educate the nation's students and to prepare them for competition in an increasingly global workforce.[1] In response to these accusations of regress and decreasing student performances, state-level and national-level reforms have called for implementing academic standards to which schools and students must be held accountable. A growing number of legislators and educators argue that this is the only way to guarantee progress in American schools toward the goal of educating all students successfully. Standards-based reform involves aligning teachers' instruction and student learning with statewide standards that can be measured through annual assessments of students, a process furthered by continuous professional development of teachers and principals.

Standards-based reforms have enjoyed widespread political support throughout the nation. The administrations of the past four presidents have moved increasingly to promote such changes at the national level. Goals 2000 under Bill Clinton called for students to be first in the world

---

1. Although there probably is some merit to these critics' claims, it is important to note that many researchers do not hold to the contention that public schooling in the United States is failing our students (see Berends, Lucas, Sullivan, & Briggs, 2005; Berliner & Biddle, 1995; Grissmer, Kirby, Berends, & Williamson, 1994; Rothstein, 1998).

on science and mathematics tests by the year 2000, and George W. Bush's No Child Left Behind Act of 2001 (NCLB) expanded the role of standardized tests to evaluate schools' progress in educating their students with the aim that all students would be proficient in reading and mathematics by 2014. Although NCLB has generated widespread debate, its initial passage in Congress showed the strong bipartisan support for the use of standards-based accountability. At the core of these reforms across the country is a focus on students and the conviction that they must be able to demonstrate what they have learned in their course work by performing on various assessments at different points in their academic careers.

Standards-based reform consists of four key elements: content and performance standards, curriculum and instructional alignment, assessments, and accountability.

Content and Performance Standards

Content standards answer the question, what should students know and be able to do? These goals consist of key concepts, facts, and skills that students are expected to learn in school. States often express these in the forms of what a student should be able to understand, do, or know at every grade level and every subject. These standards vary in complexity, content, and detail. Educators have established the standards by determining reasonable benchmarks that students of each age should meet. Students are expected to meet an increasingly higher and more complex set of standards that build upon previous concepts, skills, and facts.

Performance standards refer to how well students should know the content. Such standards consist of the goals or benchmarks that students are expected to meet. Typically, these are measured with the use of assessments to establish different performance levels, such as whether students are below basic, basic, or proficient.

Many of these basic ideas are not new to education: Teachers and schools have long set various benchmarks for their students to learn in classes and subject areas. The big difference with the current reforms is that the new standards are now used on statewide bases rather than within specific classes, schools, or districts. All students within a state are expected to meet the state-set standards by a certain age or grade, and all students are expected to demonstrate this by their performance on various statewide evaluations.

Curriculum Alignment

A second key element of standards-based reform is the *alignment of the delivered curriculum* to the standards. Alignment entails focusing teaching and instruction to match the priorities set forth by statewide standards. Schools and teachers must respond to the learning priorities set forth in the standards by emphasizing those same skills, concepts, and content in their curricula. For students to meet the state standards, school districts across the country are aiming to align curricular textbooks and materials to those benchmarks. By virtue of these requirements, standards have begun to push widespread change in curricula as they indicate what is important for students to learn and be able to do at particular ages in particular subjects. Support for such alignment stems from international studies that described the U.S. curriculum as "a mile wide and an inch deep," which was based in large part on analyses of U.S. math and science textbooks (Porter, 2002; Schmidt et al., 2001; Schmidt, McKnight, & Raizen, 1997). In addition, the emphasis on curricular alignment is based on a number of research studies showing that teaching focused on content aligned to standards and assessments is associated with higher test scores (e.g., Brophy & Good, 1986; Gamoran, Porter, Smithson, & White, 1997; Knapp, Shields, & Turnbull, 1992; Newmann & Wehlage, 1995; Wong, Hedges, Borman, & D'Agostino, 1996). Some research has begun to document this trend in which standards serve as change agents to direct teachers' improvement of content organization (McGeehee & Griffith, 2001). Although some contend that teachers may be aligning their content and instruction too narrowly to meet the requirements of the assessments (Hamilton, Stecher, & Klein, 2002), the aim of aligning curriculum to standards is a critical quest on which many schools and districts across the nation are embarking.

Assessment and Accountability

This brings us to *assessment,* the third key component of these reforms. Like the standards themselves, the assessments that states have implemented to test student performance according to the standards have ranged greatly. However, under NCLB legislation, every child in grades 3–8 must be tested every year in reading, math, and science. States typically assess students once during the spring of each school year. State assessments are supposed to match or align with individual state standards. As such, a key question that drives the assessments is, to what extent have students mastered the standards? It is not sufficient under NCLB to answer this question in terms of all students, on average. Rather, states and districts must report the percentage of students tested and the percentage of students proficient, that is, passing the benchmark, disaggregated by the following subgroups: all students, major ethnic and racial groups, limited English proficient, economically disadvantaged, migrant, gender, and students with disabilities.

Once test scores have been calculated, they are disseminated to various organizations throughout the state, both inside and outside of education. States and districts receiving Title I funds must prepare and disseminate annual report cards according to NCLB.

The disaggregated results on the state standardized tests are used to determine if a school has met *adequate yearly progress* (AYP) under No Child Left Behind. Each state defines adequate yearly progress for school districts and schools by setting the level of student achievement a school must attain for each of the subgroups (http://www.ed.gov/nclb/accountability/schools/accountability.html). AYP measures the yearly progress toward achieving grade-level performance for each student group. These report cards contain such information as depicted in Tables 1.1 and 1.2.

The information is made public to provide *accountability*, the last element of standards-based reform. Reformers argue that scores on these standardized tests offer evidence of the degree to which teachers, classes, or schools have made progress in educating students according to the standards and benchmarks. Accountability entails monitoring, challenging, and rewarding educators to improve student learning as evidenced on standardized assessments. To promote enforcement of this accountability, standardized test scores are made public through newspaper articles, local news organizations, and state or district Web site postings. As performance-based pay has yet to become a pervasive policy, public knowledge comprises some of the most widespread incentives and pressures for educators to improve their students' performance.

Depending on the state, these test scores are then used as criteria in various decisions. Tests that are used to make critical decisions about rewards and sanctions for districts, schools, students, or teachers are called *high-stakes tests*. For example, in many states students must pass high school tests to graduate; in other states test scores may be tied to pay raises. The stakes associated with such test results are high, and they may go only higher.

NCLB ties schools' receipt of national-level funding for certain programs to their students' performances on state standardized tests. Such policies have increased pressure on principals and teachers to improve student scores on these assessments. The use of standardized test scores in these ways is designed to give educators multiple incentives to improve students' performances and thereby improve their learning as defined by the benchmarks. Reformers argue that such policies will not only promote improved student learning but also offer educators and others a complex way of monitoring progress toward the standards.

Key to implementing standards-based reform is *high-quality professional development*. Within the context of standards-based reform, professional development is the mechanism that effective leaders use to help

Table 1.1 Grades K–8: Subgroup Disaggregation for Math Scores

Math

Criterion-Reference Test (CRT)	Year One			Year Two						Year Two State					
	% Below Proficient	% Proficient & Advanced	% Proficient & Advanced 2 Year Average	% Tested (Target 95%)	% Below Proficient	% Proficient (Target Proficient & Advanced 79%)	% Advanced	% Proficient & Advanced 2 Year Average	% Proficient & Advanced 3 Year Average	% Tested (Target 95%)	% Below Proficient	% Proficient (Target Prof & Adv 79%)	% Advanced (Target Prof & Adv 79%)	% Proficient & Advanced 2 Year Average	% Proficient & Advanced 3 Year Average
All Students	24.0	76.0	75.0	100	19.0	51.0	30.0	79.0	77.0	100	12.0	48.0	40.0	86.0	83.0
White	15.0	85.0	85.0	100	11.0	44.0	45.0	87.0	86.0	100	8.0	45.0	47.0	91.0	89.0
Hispanic	29.0	71.0	68.0	99	23.0	57.0	20.0	74.0	71.0	100	19.0	53.0	28.0	79.0	76.0
African American	33.0	67.0	66.0	100	25.0	57.0	18.0	71.0	69.0	100	23.0	57.0	20.0	73.0	70.0
Native American	18.0	82.0	80.0	100	11.0	50.0	39.0	86.0	83.0	100	12.0	50.0	38.0	87.0	84.0
Asian/Pacific Islander	13.0	87.0	86.0	100	6.0	38.0	56.0	91.0	89.0	100	4.0	32.0	64.0	95.0	93.0
Economically Disadvantaged	33.0	67.0	66.0	100	25.0	56.0	19.0	71.0	69.0	100	19.0	56.0	25.0	78.0	75.0
Students With Disabilities	67.0	33.0	28.0	99	54.0	37.0	9.0	40.0	34.0	99	45.0	42.0	13.0	50.0	46.0
Limited English Proficient	46.0	54.0	52.0	99	29.0	54.0	17.0	63.0	58.0	100	26.0	53.0	21.0	70.0	67.0
Female					18.0	53.0	29.0				11.0	50.0	39.0		
Male					21.0	49.0	30.0				13.0	47.0	40.0		
Migrant											30.0	54.0	16.0		
Nonmigrant					19.0	51.0	30.0				12.0	48.0	40.0		

SOURCE: Department of Education, Tennessee.

Table 1.2 Disaggregated Results for High School Students Meeting Adequate Yearly Progress

High School	All	White	Hispanic	African American	Native American
Math					
% Tested	+	+	+	+	<45
% Proficient/ Advanced	x	+	x	x	<45
Reading, Language Arts, Writing					
% Tested	+	+	+	+	<45
% Proficient/ Advanced	+	+	+	+	<45
Event Dropout Rate	+				
Met AYP?	x				

High School	Asian/ Pacific Islander	Economic Disadvantaged	Students w/ Disabilities	Limited English Proficient
Math				
% Tested	+	+	+	+
% Proficient/ Advanced	+	x	x	x
Reading, Language Arts, Writing				
% Tested	+	+	+	+
% Proficient/ Advanced	+	x	+	x
Event Dropout Rate				
Met AYP?				

SOURCE: Department of Education, Tennessee.

Key: + = meets AYP; x = does not meet AYP

teachers learn and understand new content standards. Professional development also drives the implementation of rigorous standards-based reform by helping teachers implement curriculum and pedagogy that help all students meet the standards.

Research has documented many elements that are associated with highly effective professional development for teachers (Desimone, Garet, Birman, Porter, & Yoon, 2002; Desimone, Porter, Garet, Yoon, & Birman, 2002; Garet, Porter, Desimone, Birman, & Yoon, 2001; Knapp, Copland, & Talbert, 2003). Perhaps one of the important characteristics of high-quality professional development is that it is sustained over time and linked to schoolwide improvement efforts. Teachers are actively involved in planning and setting goals for their own learning. Effective professional development focuses on both content (e.g., math or literacy) and pedagogy. Furthermore, it provides opportunities for ongoing support, feedback, and assistance for implementation of change. High-quality professional development is aligned to state and district standards and assessments.

VIGNETTE REVISITED

The vignette at the outset of the chapter provides a picture of a realistic, yet challenging, scenario facing many school principals. While considering the challenges facing a new leader at Rosemont School, reflect upon your own professional development experiences. In what ways have professional development experiences prepared you to meet the Rosemont challenges? What types of professional development might you seek to better equip you to meet these kinds of issues?

Principals play a key role in both planning and delivering professional development to teachers. By supporting and developing a school context and culture for teacher learning through collaboration and support, principals have a profound impact on teacher professional development (Gamoran et al., 2003). In this role, data-based decision-making knowledge is part of the repertoire for school principals. They can help teachers use data to identify individual students who need remedial assistance, tailor instruction to individual students' needs, identify and correct gaps in the curriculum, improve or increase the involvement of parents in student learning, and assign or reassign students to classes or groups. Furthermore, data can help teachers identify areas where they need to strengthen their own content knowledge or teaching skills—in other words, where to focus professional development.

This section has described the key components of standards-based reform and its role in data-based decision making. In the next section we review some of the research on standards-based reform and its links to student performance.

What Do We Know About Standards-Based Reform?

The core premise of standards-based reform is that by aligning the key elements of the system—expectations for what students should know, assessments of how well students know the content, curriculum alignment to standards, professional development for teachers, and accountability for performance—we can build a more coherent and powerful education system (Fuhrman & Elmore, 2004; Porter, 1994; Smith & O'Day, 1991; Vinovskis, 1996). However, research on the effects of alignment on student learning to high standards remains an open question. We know little about whether aligning the key elements of standards-based reform are affecting student learning as policymakers and educators intend (Porter, 2002). Some acknowledge that standards-based reforms have pushed teachers to clarify their goals and use a range of instructional strategies to help diverse students in their classrooms. However, they also worry about evidence that the initiatives have caused teachers to embrace techniques that are detrimental to student learning, such as lockstep curricula and retention or promotion decisions based on a single test (Falk, 2002).

Research studies that examine the alignment of state tests to state standards (Council of Chief State School Officers, 2005; Porter, 2002; Rothman, Slattery, Vranek, & Resnick, 2002; Webb, 1997) reveal that, generally, state assessments are only weakly aligned to standards. In addition, the lack of alignment is due to the tests' emphasis on facts, recall, and routine procedures and not on understanding and interpretation. As such, there are significant challenges that remain for standards-based accountability in America's schools. However, as standards-based reform continues to unfold in schools across the nation, it is imperative to provide support to schools to use the data at hand to improve curriculum, instruction, professional development, and overall alignment of the educational program.

WHY DATA-BASED DECISION MAKING?

Continuous Improvement

Although data-driven decision making is a buzz phrase in educational leadership circles today, it has deep theoretical origins in the organizational-theory literature on continuous improvement and learning curves (Zangwill & Kantor, 1998).

The origins of continuous improvement can be traced back to the early 1950s when Toyota implemented a *just-in-time* improvement strategy in which employees would conduct routine weekly analyses to improve their job performance (Adler, 1991). In education, continuous improvement can be an integral part of standards-based reform if test scores and other accountability information are used for organizational learning. "Because organizations learn from experience incrementally in response to feedback about outcomes, the increase in the sheer volume of information provided by a strengthened state accountability system may provide the experience necessary for higher-level learning" (Coggshall, 2004, p. 9).

Organizational learning is the process by which members of an organization, schools in our case, acquire and use information to change and implement action (Dixon, 1999). Organizational learning occurs as a social and dynamic process. Organizational learning occurs when knowledge is distributed across individuals and is embedded in the culture, values, and routines of the organization. This type of learning is a developmental process that can occur in an organization over time.

Data can serve as a catalyst to propel organizational learning. As will be explained later, data refer to multiple sources and types of information. Although many think of scores on standardized tests as the main type of data, other data include information about the students, school programs, and others measures of student learning such as student work, ongoing formative assessments, and portfolios. Data are not limited to students and programs. Data include observations of the quality of teaching and the content of the curriculum actually taught in the classroom.

School leaders can use data to develop a culture of learning for adults as well as students in the school with the regular flow of information from data. Leaders can use data to put into place mechanisms to support individual and collective learning surrounding data by pursuing such questions as: What are the data telling us? What can we learn from the data? How can we change our practice in light of the data? What other data do we need to collect? How does the information from standardized assessments compare with teachers' grades and other more local information about student performance and development? Ideally, teacher teams have access to information that is used to build collaborative relationships and drive cycles of inquiry. Therefore, data that is dispersed and shared throughout the school will better facilitate the professional climate and organizational learning. In fact, for data to be useful to the organization, there should be a number of teams in place that can facilitate the data-driven processes.

Accountability

Perhaps one of the most widespread reasons that data-based decision making is so important for school leaders is new accountability mechanisms in schools. With standards-based reform, targets are set for what students are to achieve, the standards, and schools are held accountable for reaching those targets. Educational reform rests clearly at the foot of school accountability. Much of the accountability that school leaders encounter is *external accountability*. This is often referred to as bureaucratic or political accountability as each person or level in the organizational hierarchy is held accountable by a superior at the next level in the organization: principals to superintendents, teachers to principals, and school systems to the boards of education. NCLB is an example of external accountability where benchmarks and standards are determined by those outside the school site, such as the state and federal governing bodies. NCLB has focused accountability on student outcomes and school performance. In these instances school leaders must use data to answer the questions: Have I met the standards imposed on us? Are all students making adequate yearly progress? What proportion of students score at or about proficiency levels as determined by state tests? Is our school meeting graduation targets? In this sense data are used to report and comply with regulations from local, state, and federal agencies.

NCLB has changed markedly the use of data-based decision making in two fundamental ways. First, there is now an abundance of data available for schools and their leaders to analyze. NCLB mandates annual testing for all students in Grades 3–8. Many states also mandate high school exit examinations as a requirement for graduation. Consequently, at a minimum there are data regarding performance levels. Other data reported under NCLB often include attendance and graduation rates. Therefore, data are available much more than they were in the past. Many districts and schools use these data to set improvement goals and targets.

Second, as noted earlier, NCLB has created an accountability climate where there are incentives and sanctions for student progress toward achievement goals. Thus the importance of using data for school improvement is much more central than it was in the past. There is increasing pressure on schools to meet student achievement goals for *all* students. Using the available data for decisions is no longer a matter of leadership preference; it is a key tool for meeting accountability responsibilities.

However, a second type of accountability is *market accountability*. Market accountability is implemented through school-choice programs where schools are held accountable by the market—parents will choose "good" schools. School choice refers to programs that enable parents to select the schools their children attend, thereby freeing them from mandatory attendance at schools defined by catchment areas. There are several school-choice programs in the public school arena where parents do not pay tuition and can choose among public school options. Public school-choice programs include interdistrict and intradistrict transfer programs, open enrollment, charter schools, and magnet schools. More recent choice programs include vouchers. Most school-choice plans, even those in the public school arena, are based on a market orientation toward school improvement. It is assumed that parents will choose schools and schools will exhibit some level of responsiveness to meet the various needs and preferences of their "clients" (i.e., students and their parents; Chubb & Moe, 1990). According to the theory of voice and exit, if schools fail to respond to parental dissatisfaction, parents will enroll their children elsewhere (Hirschman, 1970). It would follow that schools will then improve in order to compete to attract parents and students.

Public school choice has been given new prominence by NCLB, which requires that students in failing schools be given the option to transfer to more successful schools in their districts. This is in keeping with other provisions of the act that seek to strengthen accountability in public education. The prospect of losing students is meant to operate as a sanction to spur failing schools to improve. However, this is not the only purpose served by this provision of the law. Advocates of expanded choice in public education do not see choice merely as a sanction. Choice is also viewed as a mechanism for creating more successful schools, particularly in communities where low income makes it difficult for parents to exercise options available to the more affluent, who choose better schools by changing residential location (see Belfield & Levin, 2005; Henig, 1999). In theory and in practice, school choice and market accountability require widespread use of data. Data are used by consumers, both parents and students, when making school choices. Data are used by schools to compare themselves with "competitors" and continually improve to attract parents and students. And data are used by external regulators, such as those who grant and revoke charters.

Although uniformly implemented and externally imposed accountability systems are gaining the most attention, a third type of accountability is the *internal accountability* of schools, emphasizing school workplace norms; local decision making; and school goals, assessments, and consequences. Internal accountability is different from external or market accountability in that local groups of educators develop performance standards based on professional judgment. Data are used as internal assessments to monitor instruction and progress toward school-based standards. Internal accountability is touted by some as a more effective means to changing classroom practices because "Teachers' motivation originates inside the schools, where their collaboration can affect teaching directly" (Adams & Kirst, 1999, p. 485). In the domain of accountability, the challenges for educational leaders are twofold. First, educational leaders must play a key role in articulating and setting standards and measures of accountability while aligning local expectations and accountability with external frameworks. Second, leaders need to engage teachers in meaningful, collaborative discourse around standards and measures while providing professional development opportunities and other supports to help them meet established goals (Newmann, 2002; Newmann & Associates, 1996).

VIGNETTE REVISITED

If you were the new principal at Rosemont Middle School, how would you go about constructing a data-gathering and data-analysis plan? In other words, if you had to provide a chronological list of data to be collected and analyzed, along with an accompanying rationale for why the particular data were important, what would such a document or plan look like? Further, in what manner would you involve additional school personnel and stakeholders in this process?

Focus Efforts and Monitor Progress

Even though using data to respond to and monitor internal and external accountability is necessary, data-based decision making also drives strategic plans and resource allocation. Data are used to evaluate policies and programs and to develop and improve curriculum, teaching, and learning. In this case data are used to continually guide improvement, and thus engaging with data is not an end-of-the-year occurrence. Data are lynchpins in planning and implementing focused improvement strategies. Multiple types and sources of data are used to understand the school's strengths and weaknesses, set priorities, focus change efforts, and establish a baseline from which to monitor progress.

Build Community Through Organizational Learning

An emerging view of teaching, referred to as the *new professionalism* of teaching, conceptualizes teaching as part of a communal endeavor, moving "away from the teachers' traditional professional authority and autonomy towards new forms of relationships with colleagues, with students and with parents. These relationships are becoming closer as well as more intense and collaborative" (Hargreaves, 1994, p. 424). Similarly,

Darling-Hammond (1997) have studied high-performing schools, schools that are successful in sustaining learning for all children, especially children that traditionally fail. The school climate or environment of such high-performing schools is characterized as "caring-forms of organization that enable close, sustained relationship amongst students and teachers" (p. 148). Data can be an important lever for creating and supporting professional relationships and community in schools through collective, organizational learning.

Data offer an opportunity to bridge the divide that often exists between schools and parents. As schools are required to communicate more information about their students to the community at large, deeper dialogue between educators and parents can also occur. This relationship works in both directions: Parents can understand more about their children's academic achievements, and educators can gain a broader understanding of their students' backgrounds. In an evaluation of the *Children Achieving School Program* in Philadelphia public schools, the Consortium for Policy Research in Education documented how the program included parents in setting learning standards to evaluate student progress in different subject areas. Parents reported a deeper understanding and appreciation for the curricula and a greater sense of inclusion in the school. Educators for their part described an appreciation for the contributions many parents made to the process (Golds, Rhodes, Brown, Lytle, & Waff, 2001). In addition to the increased communication that comes through publicizing certain data such as standardized tests, educators can use data to encourage parental involvement in their children's education.

CONCLUSION

With the increased use of test scores for different decisions has come the need to understand just what the data actually mean. As educators face the growing importance and prevalence of standardized tests, it is imperative that they know how to analyze and then *use* the data resulting from these tests. Moreover, as the discussion and research about standardized test scores deepen, it is important that educators lead the dialogue about what exactly comprises true learning and how to develop multiple sources and types of data to help drive instructional improvement and evaluate it. How can we use testing data to improve student learning? What other measures can help a school monitor progress it is making in teaching its students? Who is succeeding on the tests, and who is failing? What policies and practices do schools change in response to the data they collect? Though the debate about standardized testing has increased with the growth of these assessments, educators must, nonetheless, recognize the increasing value of data and the need to obtain a greater literacy of data analysis and decision making because they are the best positioned to use such information to improve student learning.

Standards-based reform is encouraging educators everywhere to include data analysis skills in their repertoire as they search for ways to monitor and improve school and student progress according to standards. These initiatives mandate that educators set specific goals for student performance and then monitor student progress and success toward those benchmarks. Assessment of this progress means collecting data, evaluating it, and then using the results to modify school policies or classroom curriculum and instruction to attain achievement goals. Greater accountability for schools, classrooms, and individual teachers has pushed data-analysis responsibilities from district and state levels to individual school faculties.

It is the need to understand how to *use* data to inform practice, rather than merely collect it and pass it on to others that is the key to data-based decision making.

Without analyzing and discussing data, schools are unlikely to identify and solve the problems that need attention, identify appropriate interventions to solve those problems, or know how they are progressing toward achievement of their goals. Data are the fuel of reform. In short, using data separates good schools from mediocre schools. Schools that are increasing student achievement, staff productivity and collegiality, and community satisfaction use data to inform and guide their decisions and actions. Data essentially sets a course of action and keeps a staff on that course to school improvement and student success (Jandris, 2001).

Despite the growing acceptance of data-based decision making, adopting these new skills and attitudes is not easy, and many obstacles exist. These include a lack of data-analysis skills, "antidata" cultures that might exist in schools, too little time to address the issue in teaching schedules that are already stretched thin, a lack of technical and financial resources, and an absence of shared vision for its value or implementation. Principal and teacher leaders must recognize these limitations and work with and through them if they are to promote data-based decision making successfully within their faculties. Implementing this new paradigm for school improvement entails not only a profound change in vision for how a school thinks about itself but also a concerted effort to equip personnel with the skills and resources to pursue such a goal. These perspectives can lead educators toward developing schools that are effective for all students. But what are the components of effective schools? It is to this subject we turn in the next chapter.

Discussion Questions

1. Briefly describe one benefit and one challenge associated with each of the four components of standards-based reform.

2. Why is data-based decision making so important to meet the needs of all children?

3. In the chapter, four reasons for data-driven decision making were discussed. Choose one of these four reasons and explain how you have seen data used in a way that facilitated this purpose.

4. Before the discussion of effective schools in the next chapter, briefly describe your thoughts about what characteristics make schools effective for all students.

Data for School Improvement

The underlying purpose of using data is the improvement of the educational experiences of all students. As such, it is imperative that school leaders understand the various ways in which school improvement can be gauged. At the end of this chapter, you should understand the key indicators of school improvement as well as the manner in which data can inform processes aimed at enhancing the educational experiences of students.

VIGNETTE REVISITED

As the new principal of Rosemont School immersed in the many challenges of raising the achievement of all students in your school, you now understand some issues related to standards-based reform and the importance of data-based decision making. You know that you need to understand the data on your school and systematically examine your school's activities as a leader for school improvement. Although you are committed to these general issues, you have some concerns about how this commitment is carried out—by you, your staff, parents, students, and community. For you to craft a meaningful path toward school improvement, what aspects of your school need to be examined, and what types of data need to be analyzed?

The critical question addressed in this chapter is, what are the pathways to creating successful schools with data? The paths are many, but fortunately they share some common themes. The anchor for effective school improvement efforts is a schoolwide focus on teaching and learning. Toward that end, school leaders need to attend to the school's mission and goals, rigorous content standards for all students, curricular and instructional coherence and alignment, expert teachers supported by high-quality professional development, the professional community of teachers, the climate of the school, the relationship of schools to their families and community, and the allocation of resources to goals.

This chapter discusses each of these themes, their interrelationships, and the importance of gathering data on these pathways to enhance school improvement and student learning. The indicators or pathways identify important types of data that are essential to data-based decision making. Often school leaders feel overwhelmed by the amounts of data at their disposal; they often do not know how to decide which data to collect. What data are most important? No Child Left Behind requires accountability for student performance and makes available data on student achievement and other indicators such as attendance and graduation rates. However, these data alone are not sufficient for data-based decision making. They can provide information about some student outcomes, but they do not provide sufficient information about how schools and their students can improve. Data regarding student learning *and* the indicators or pathways to school improvement are essential.

Before discussing these school improvement indicators in turn, we provide a brief description of the research that reveals their importance in schools today. Subsequent chapters will discuss the specific data used to measure student achievement and learning outcomes as well as the data used to measure the pathways to effective schools. Our aim in this chapter is to provide a framework for thinking about data and the multiple indicators for school improvement efforts. In ensuing chapters we discuss specific measures of achievement and school-improvement pathways.

RESEARCH ON EFFECTIVE SCHOOLS

For decades educators have been concerned about how effectively we are teaching the nation's youth. More than 50 years ago, when the Soviets launched Sputnik in 1957, the United States was suddenly scrambling to reclaim its place as a technological leader. One step toward this recovery was a strong commitment to investing in the public education system. If human capital was to promote productivity, and thereby advance our struggle against communism, where was the acquisition of knowledge and skills generated? For many the answer was in school.

At about the same time, the civil rights movement drew educational researchers into studies of social inequality. There were questions to answer about the quality of education provided to students of color and those living in poverty compared to that provided to white middle-class children. There was a wide gap in their academic achievement scores, dropout rates, educational attainment levels, and the schooling conditions. During this era the importance of individual background characteristics and its impact on educational experiences and accomplishments became an area of focus.

With the publication of the Coleman and colleagues' *Equality of Educational Opportunity* report in 1966—aimed at understanding how schools affected students' learning opportunities, particularly those who have been historically disadvantaged—we learned that the effects of school resources (size, location, per pupil expenditures, library books, science laboratories, and guidance counselors) did not explain the differential achievement between lower class and middle class, and minority and majority white students. Coleman and others found that, when controlling for characteristics of students' social backgrounds (e.g., socioeconomic, racial-ethnic, gender), differences between schools in terms of their resources had little relationship to students' academic achievement. We also learned that the differences in student achievement within schools were much greater than those between schools.

This research was not without its critics. Many claimed that Coleman and colleagues failed to look inside schools and understand the processes that occurred there (Barr & Dreeben, 1983; Karabel & Halsey, 1977). Thus subsequent research began to examine the organizational features of schooling that explained the variation of outcomes within schools, which was greater than the variation between schools (see Bidwell & Friedkin, 1988; Dreeben, 1994; Hallinan, Gamoran, Kubitschek, & Loveless, 2003).

Another response involved examination of additional organizational features of schools thought to improve student learning, particularly for students from high-poverty settings. Much of this research relied on methods that compared schools that were performing higher than expected to those that were low performing. Relying on case studies to examine these schools in more detail, researchers revealed the distinguishing characteristics of effective schools.

Highlighted by the research of Ron Edmonds in the late 1970s, this body of work set forth the foundation for the "Effective Schools Movement." Edmonds listed five ingredients, or correlates, of effective schools: strong leadership, high expectations for children's achievement, a safe and orderly school climate and environment conducive to learning, an emphasis on basic skills, and frequent monitoring of pupil progress. Edmonds' research led directly to an organized movement that affected many schools. Furthermore, these factors were the early precursors to our understanding of continuous school improvement today.

The Effective Schools Movement and its research have developed over time and have continued to reveal school-level factors that are positively related to student achievement. Important effective schools characteristics include school leadership from principals and teachers that focuses on a sense of community with a clear mission, goals, and high expectations commonly shared throughout the school; maximizing learning time on instructional issues to engage students in academic work; a stable and committed staff; a planned purposeful program of courses that focuses on academic development; ongoing schoolwide staff development and training; schoolwide recognition of academic success; ongoing and stable district support; a culture within the school that involves collaborative planning time among teachers; strong parent involvement and participation in the education of their children and the life of the school; and an orderly environment (e.g., reasonable rules that are fairly and consistently enforced to minimize problems of a noisy, disruptive, and unsafe learning environment; Comer, 1980; Edmonds, 1979; Masden, 1994; Purkey & Smith, 1983; Rutter, Maughan, Mortimore, Ouston, & Smith, 1979). Highly relevant to our discussion of data-driven decision making is the emphasis on continuous monitoring of student progress as an effective school practice.

One issue that continues to challenge educators is that although researchers can point to effective schools, it is difficult to understand the school-improvement pathways to *become* effective (Berends, 2004). Helping readers understand the components of effective schools and providing insights about how to use data to develop effective schooling processes is our aim in this chapter.

STANDARDS-BASED REFORM AND SCHOOL IMPROVEMENT

In the last chapter, we outlined the key elements of standards-based reform. The underlying theory of the standards-based reform policies is fairly straightforward:

> The centerpiece of the system is a set of challenging standards. By setting these standards for all students, states would hold high expectations for performance; these expectations would be the same regardless of students' backgrounds or where they attended school. Aligned assessments to the standards would allow

students, parents, and teachers to monitor student performance against the standards. Providing flexibility to schools would permit them to make the instructional and structural changes needed for their students to reach the standards. And holding schools accountable for meeting the standards would create incentives to redesign instruction toward the standards and provide appropriate assistance to schools that need extra help. (National Research Council, 1999, pp. 2–3)

However, these policies are unlikely to affect student learning unless they are linked directly to efforts to build both teacher and school capacity. It has long been recognized that meaningful change cannot take place in educational institutions without changes being made to the core technology of schooling, namely, teaching and learning (see Gamoran, Nystrand, Berends, & LePore, 1995; Oakes, Gamoran, & Page, 1992). However, today there is a greater understanding that clear standards and strong incentives by themselves are not sufficient to change teaching and learning. Instead, there needs to be a focus on "capacity-building", that is, building those elements needed to support effective instruction (Massell, 1998). To build this capacity, it is critical to support professional development that improves teachers' knowledge and skills, provide appropriate curriculum frameworks and materials, and organize and allocate resources through strategic school-improvement planning. In the next section we present key indicators of school improvement that serve as the building blocks, or pathways, of developing a school's capacity for continuous improvement.

Key Indicators of School Improvement

The remainder of this chapter provides specific indicators to make schooling more effective. Understanding the key indicators of school improvement and how data can inform processes toward improvement goals is important as schools face overwhelming demands and an over-abundance of data. These indicators are the building blocks of a school's capacity for continuous improvement. The specific school-improvement indicators we discuss include:

- Shared mission and goals
- Rigorous content standards for all students agreed upon, understood, and measurable
- Alignment to standards—curriculum and instructional coherence
- Expert teachers supported by coherent, consistent professional development
- Professional community

- Partnerships with parents, families, and community
- Culture and climate for student learning
- Resources aligned to goals
- Data-based processes for analyzing programs, practices, and results

The specific school-improvement indicators we focus on begin with the shared mission and goals of the school that must be aligned with state standards. We then discuss other school-improvement indicators, including rigorous standards that are agreed upon, understood, and measurable; curriculum and instruction aligned to standards; expert teachers supported by coherent, consistent professional development; professional community; partnerships with parents and community resources; culture and climate for student learning; and resources aligned to goals. We end this chapter with a discussion of the importance of data-based processes for analyzing programs, practices, and results, which is key to informing all of the other school-improvement indicators. It is crucial for data to be collected, analyzed, and discussed for each of these school-improvement indicators, or what we call *pathways*, as part of the continuous planning process. In this chapter we briefly provide examples of how data can be used regarding each of the improvement indicators. In Chapter 6 we provide specific details regarding data for each pathway, or indicator.

Figure 2.1 portrays the interrelationships of these effective school indicators, or pathways, with the school mission and goals as the center, the other indicators supporting that mission, and the entire school-improvement set of processes supported by a foundation on continuous data-based decision making. What should be clear from Figure 2.1 is that the indicators are all interrelated. Leaders can look at features of effective schools as a bundle of schooling activities and processes, overlapping and mutually supportive. At the foundation, however, is the use of data-based processes for analyzing programs, practices, and results regarding each of the indicators as well as the actual measurements of the key goal of schooling: student performance, learning, and achievement.

Shared Mission and Goals

For decades researchers have pointed to the importance of school mission and goals in guiding the activities of schools. Shared mission and goals are the extent to which principals and teachers establish educational priorities and clear sets of academic activities to accomplish school goals. Moreover, staff members agree about the school mission and goals and commitment to them (Louis, Marks, & Kruse, 1996; Newmann et al., 1996). The challenge for establishing meaningful missions, however, has been to establish goals, priorities, and supporting activities that provide substantive direction for the activities in the school. When discussing the importance of shared goals, Newmann (2002) writes:

> Staff in effective schools use a common language directed toward a specific intellectual mission, rather than vague slogan such as "All students can learn." There is continuous debate and inquiry about how best to achieve the school's intellectual mission. For example, before adopting proposed new techniques of teaching, assessment of student learning or new programs for student support, teachers inquire critically about the potential of new practices to elevate the intellectual quality of student work. (pp. 28–29)

Figure 2.1 Key Indicators of School Improvement

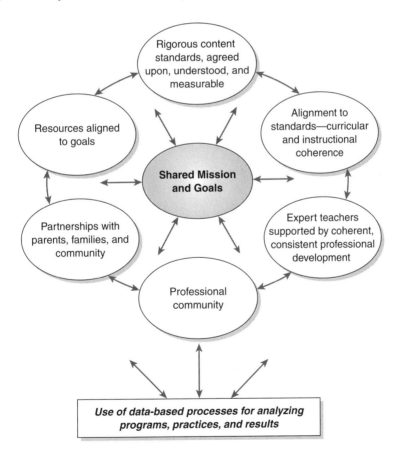

VIGNETTE REVISITED

Recall the situation at Rosemont School, which requires a systematic analysis of the school's activities with an eye towards school improvement. Comment on the merits of utilizing Figure 2.1 as a framework for organizing the important task of examining key aspects of the school related to school improvement.

As noted by Hawley and Sykes (2007), values play a key role in determining goals of learning, and achieving consensus around them. Clarifying values among key stakeholders can reduce conflicts and ambiguity. Furthermore, it is more important to focus on small sets of key goals with broad consensus rather than developing a long laundry list of goals with little agreement.

Data play a central role in the goal-setting process, as will be further explained in the next chapter. It is important during the goal-setting process to determine agreed-upon evidence that schools will routinely collect and use to monitor progress toward reaching their goals and to help them diagnose areas for improvement. Data are central to the process of goal benchmarking—identifying and analyzing performance, practices, and processes. Only through data can the school and its community know if they are achieving their goals.

Rigorous Content Standards for All Students: Agreed Upon, Understood, and Measurable

Effective schools have a shared mission and goals focusing on student learning. Effective schools concentrate on achievement goals aimed at a shared understanding of and continuous commitment to challenging academic standards for what students should know.

Within the context of current educational policies, the depth and specificity of state and district standards varies widely (Porter, 2002). That is, the extent to which the standards provide detailed guidance to help schools and teachers understand what it is they are supposed to teach varies widely by state and by subject areas. Because of this variation, some state and district standards are seen as more legitimate and as having the support of those responsible for implementation and thereby have greater influence on teachers. For instance, standards may have the backing of the state as developed by a consensus process throughout the educational community and also have the support of teachers within a given school. Such standards are likely to have more authority (Clune, 1998; Porter, 1994). The standards are also likely to be seen as legitimate by teachers if they report that the standards are challenging for students.

The depth, specificity, and authority of standards have implications for effective teaching in schools. Effective schools research has shown that schools striving for high levels of student learning have teachers who dedicate themselves to the quality of curricular content, accuracy and precision in teaching practices and student performance, and in-depth understanding of instructional practice and student achievement (see Newmann, 2002; Newmann et al., 1996; Newmann & Wehlage, 1995).

In spite of the variation in state standards and the overwhelming amounts of modern knowledge, teachers in effective schools are able to make decisions about what knowledge is substantively worth teaching, provide depth and specificity to the academic standards to guide their instruction, and ensure that their decisions are grounded in respectable research and data-based decision making. Moreover, when teaching the content—involving facts, theories, concepts, algorithms, question and answer sessions, and discussions—successful teachers focus on being accurate and precise. "They emphasize and celebrate 'getting it right'" (Newmann, 2002, p. 30). But getting it right does not imply learning merely isolated fragments of facts. Rather, teachers aim to move beyond the facts toward analytic, creative thinking. Students not only reconstruct the knowledge taught in the classroom but also exhibit in-depth understanding that constructs knowledge by moving beyond basic skills to synthesis and interpretation of knowledge domains. It is important to note that state standards do not always reflect this kind of teaching and learning.

Measuring this type of learning with standardized achievement tests is difficult, to say the least. A common criticism of assessments, particularly those administered in high-stakes accountability systems, has been that assessments may narrow the curriculum because teachers may limit the content they teach to that which they are being held accountable (see Hamilton et al., 2002; Heubert and Hauser, 1999; Linn, 2000; Linn, Baker, & Betebenner, 2002). This narrowing of what is taught conflicts with the type of learning discussed earlier. However, principals and teachers in effective schools can use the assessment resources at their disposal, whether through the state assessments or interim assessments, to support the school's aim of helping students attain challenging standards (Baker, 2002). We point to some of the ways that this is facilitated in the chapters that follow. The important point is to use the assessment data at hand to think critically about the instruction that is taking place to support substantive, meaningful learning.

Alignment to Standards— Curricular and Instructional Coherence

Research suggests that principals and teachers in effective schools are dedicated not only to high standards and expectations but also to expending considerable efforts on ensuring that curriculum content is aligned with state and district standards *and* assessments. This is important because state standards often do not align with state assessments. Moreover, school professionals reflect critically on their pedagogy and rely on instructional strategies identified in respectable research as being effective. In addition, when adopting school and classroom interventions and strategies, staffs in effective schools seek to make the efforts coherent and consistent across the school to support student learning (Bryk, Lee, & Holland, 1993).

Establishing such coherence and consistency across pedagogy, while ensuring content is aligned to challenging standards, involves a continuous focus on coordinating across grade levels and within grade levels. It also involves attention to the common standards of the school and ensuring coordination across subject areas, departments, and the students the school serves (Bryk et al., 1993; Newmann et al., 1996; Newmann, Smith, Allensworth, & Bryk, 2001). Moreover, schools that aim to align instruction with challenging standards rely on flexible instructional grouping arrangements that provide opportunities for all types of students to be exposed to the standards, learn them, and achieve at higher levels (Gamoran, 2004; Oakes et al., 1992). The pathway toward this coherence has many obstacles. As Fullan (1999) observed:

> It is easy to experience overload, fragmentation and incoherence. In fact, in education this is the more typical state. Policies get passed independent of each other, innovations are introduced before previous ones are adequately implemented, the sheer presence of problems and multiple unconnected solutions are overwhelming. Many schools and school systems make matters worse by indiscriminately taking on every innovation that comes along. (p. 27)

Although obstacles are many, effective schools decide on those activities that support the academic goals and mission of the school; "they are organizations that *selectively* go about learning more" (Fullan, 1999, p. 28). Principals and teachers in effective schools do not adopt every new idea, strategy, or intervention, but ask how the potential additions connect and are consistent with what they are already doing.

Expert Teachers Supported by Coherent, Consistent Professional Development

To support school missions that incorporate challenging standards that are aligned to curriculum and instruction, effective schools have teachers dedicated to developing their expertise in curriculum content and pedagogy, and create an environment that emphasizes professional learning and development for the entire organization (Darling-Hammond, 1997).

Recent research on professional development that improves student learning reveals several features that make it effective, including whether the professional development activities are more reformlike than traditional, involve a meaningful amount of time, include the entire school staff, entail a focus on the content of instruction, incorporate active learning activities, and are coherent with other aims and activities of the school (Cohen and Hill, 2000; Desimone, Porter, et al., 2002; Garet et al., 2001; Kennedy, Birman, & Demaline, 1986; Porter, Garet, Desimone, Birman, & Yoon, 2005).

Garet et al. (2001) elaborate on these professional development features that are related to improved instruction and student learning (see also Desimone, Garet, et al., 2002; Desimone, Porter, et al., 2002; Porter et al., 2003). *Reformlike* professional activities include a study group of teachers, a teacher network, mentoring relationships among staff, committee or task force participation, internships in other organizations, individual research projects, and teacher research centers. These kinds of activities contrast with more traditional forms of professional development such as workshops or conferences. The *amount of time* spent on meaningful professional development also matters for improving instruction and achievement. The number of contact hours and duration over time that participants are expected to spend on certain professional development activities is an important aspect of effective professional development. Whether the activities involve *collective participation*—the degree to which an activity emphasizes involvement of groups of principals and teachers from the same schools, departments, or grade levels—has been shown to be more effective when compared with more fragmented participation of individual teachers. Garet and colleagues' research (2001) also shows that *content focus* is an important attribute of professional development, meaning that the activity is focused on improving and deepening teachers' content knowledge in a specific subject area such as mathematics or reading. Effective professional development also involves *active learning*, that is, opportunities for teachers to become actively engaged in the meaningful analysis of teaching and learning (e.g., by reviewing student work or obtaining feedback on their teaching). Finally, Garet and colleagues show that *coherence within professional development experience is key.* Coherence refers to the degree to which a set of activities promotes coherence in teachers' professional development by encouraging continued professional communication among teachers and incorporating experiences that are consistent with school goals.

In terms of data, as noted by Hawley and Valli (2007), "Professional development should be based on collaborative analyses of the differences between (a) actual student performance and (b) goals and standards for student learning" (p. 120). The data are used to determine students' needs and align professional development to these needs. Analysis of student data, goals, and standards helps focus professional development on the most important goals and the most effective approaches to improvement rather than a menu of options or individual teacher choice. Monitoring the quantity and quality of professional development is also part of data-based decision making. The focus on data in planning and implementing professional development also reinforces the culture of organizational learning and collaborative problem solving that are core elements of continuous school improvement.

Professional Community

In addition to these overall features that research reveals are important for instruction and student learning, the alignment of these activities to challenging standards and instruction, and the continued focus on the school's mission and goals, a critical indicator for school improvement is professional community. The extent to which teachers cooperate, coordinate, and learn from each other to improve instruction and develop the curriculum is an important feature of any school embarking on the path of improvement (Louis et al., 1996).

What are effective professional communities? Judith Warren Little (2002) provides a helpful description:

> Genuine teacher learning communities—those with a demonstrable effect on teaching and learning—have a distinctive character. They question—and challenge—teaching practices when they prove ineffective with students and routinely investigate new conceptions of teaching and learning. They respect the creative contributions and passions of individuals, but are able to ask one another tough questions. Such groups maintain an open curiosity about their own practices and tolerate informed dissent. . . . As McLaughlin and Talbert (2001) observe, "teacher learning community is not simply the collection of good and committed teachers." Rather it is a group that embraces certain collective obligations for student success and well-being and that develops a certain collective expertise by employing problem solving, critique, reflection, and debate. (p. 46)

The importance of respectful, professional debate within professional learning communities is critical for continuous self-assessment—on one's own teaching practice, of one's own management of the school and classroom, of the schoolwide commitment to and engagement in furthering professional development and alignment to challenging instruction, and regarding the coherence of schooling activities with the school's mission and goals. Describing the nature of such community in effective schools, Newmann (2002) writes:

> Teachers in effective schools have common understandings of their main intellectual goals, but unanimity on intellectual mission does not entail mechanical, uniform compliance with a "party line"; routinized teaching; or a static, rigid curriculum. To the contrary, shared understanding of and collective commitment to central goals often stimulates lively faculty debate on how best to achieve the goals. Staff discussion often entails a continuous loop of asking how to improve; trying new approaches; evaluating them; and redesigning the curriculum, assessment, and teaching. This process provokes reconsideration of the goals themselves. But discussion over priorities and possible changes is conducted in ways that reinforce shared understanding and schoolwide consensus. (p. 32)

Research has demonstrated that schools organized as communities, rather than bureaucracies, are more likely to exhibit academic success (Bryk & Driscoll, 1988; Lee, Smith, & Croninger, 1995; Louis & Miles, 1990). Further research supports the notion that effective professional communities are deeply rooted in the academic and social learning goals of the schools. In other words, the communities are not for the purpose of merely creating pleasant work environments. Communities in schools must place academic learning at their center. Often termed *teacher professional communities*, these collaborative cultures are defined by elements such as shared values, focus on student learning, collaboration, deprivatized practice, and reflective dialogue (Louis et al., 1996).

As will be demonstrated in later chapters, data can help provide information regarding the extent to which teachers are engaged in teacher professional communities and how well the communities are contributing to student learning. When discussion and problem solving make extensive use of data and research-based evidence, the exchange of misconceptions and erroneous information is contained, and the discussion is more easily focused on student learning.

Partnerships With Parents, Families, and the Community

Although establishing a professional community that is dedicated to continuous assessment of schooling activities supporting high levels of learning is important, it does not happen without important partnerships with parents and community resources. Research has shown that how principals and teachers interact with the families of their students is related to the student learning that occurs. Beneficial communication activities include compacts for learning, open houses, back-to-school nights or other events scheduled for parents, home visits, communication regarding academic standards and assessments, shared goals and expectations, communication with teachers, and the provision of materials in other languages. For many of these activities, their frequency and context is important (Bryk et al., 1993; D'Agostino, Borman, Hedges, & Wong, 1998; Epstein, 1992; Muller, 1993).

There is a substantial research base that has reported positive relationships between family involvement and social and academic benefits for students (Henderson & Mapp, 2002). A study of standards-based reform practices, for instance, found that teachers' outreach to parents of low-performing students—such as meetings, sending materials home, and communicating with parents when their child was having problems—was related to improved student achievement (Westat and Policy Studies Associates, 2001). Similarly, schools with well-defined parent partnership programs show achievement gains over schools with less robust partnerships (Shaver & Wells, 1998). Community-wide involvement such as school-linked social services, parent-education programs, and community organizing initiatives aim to change the underlying conditions associated with low student achievement (Mediratta & Fruchter, 2001).

How schools help all families establish home environments to support children as students is another important feature of effective school-family communication and partnerships. Such help includes school-provided assistance with social support services, parent resource centers, designated staff to work with parents, strategies to involve parents whose native language is not English (Epstein, 1992). In addition, effective schools encourage families to be involved with children on academic activities such as sending home activities that the students and parents can work on together in reading and in math, and having parents sign homework (D'Agostino et al., 1998; Epstein, 1992).

Community partnerships are also important for effective schooling to take place. Involving the entire learning community—stakeholders, teachers, education support staff, administrators, parents, and community and business organizations—in school-improvement planning and problem solving can provide a broad base of resources to think about the school's mission, implement strategies to accomplish goals, conduct ongoing assessment to understand under what conditions strategies are effective, and engage in reflective dialogue and debate (see Hawley, 2002).

Figure 2.2 describes six dimensions, or foci, of community and family involvement. This description emerged from a synthesis of an extensive review of the literature by Epstein and colleagues (2006) at the Center on Family, School, and Community Partnerships (http://www.csos.jhu.edu/P2000/index.htm). The figure provides examples of the six dimensions of family involvement at both the eighth and twelfth grades.

Figure 2.2 Six Dimensions of Family Involvement for Grades 8 and 12

Type of Involvement	In Grade 8	In Grade 12
Parenting	– Expressing expectations about student's education – Limiting television viewing – Supervising time use and behavior	– Discussing interests, issues, and studies at school – Doing things together (shopping, vacations, movies, meals) – Supervising behavior – Knowing what courses student is taking – Supervising academic work
Communicating	– Parent-initiated contacts about academic performance – School-initiated contacts about student's academic program (courses, placement)	– School-initiated contacts about academic performance – Parent-initiated contacts on student's academic program – Parent-school contacts on post-secondary plans
Supporting school	– Volunteering at school and fund-raising	– Volunteering at school and attending school activities
Learning at home	– Academic lessons outside school – Music or dance lessons – Discussions about school and plans for future	– Encouraging college – Encouraging high school graduation – Learning about postsecondary education – Taking on private educational expenses
Decision making	– Taking part in parent organization	– Taking part in parent organization
Collaborating with community	– Using community learning resources (like museum visits) – Taking part in community	Communicating parent-to-parent

SOURCE: Epstein, J. L., et al. (2002). *Six Types of Family and Community Involvement for Grades 8 and 12*. Epstein and colleagues at the Center on Family, School, and Community Partnerships, http://www.csos.jhu.edu/P2000/index.htm

Chadwick (2004) provides the following insights about the six dimensions of family, school, and community partnerships:

1. *Parenting.* Families must provide a healthy and safe environment at home that promotes learning and good behavior at school. Schools can provide information and training to support families in this endeavor.

2. *Communicating.* Families need information about school programs and school progress in a format that meets their individual needs.

3. *Volunteering.* Families can make significant contributions to the school if schools can accommodate their schedules and interests.

4. *Learning at home.* Families can facilitate and supervise learning at home with the assistance of teachers.

5. *Decision making.* Families can have meaningful roles in the school decision-making process. This opportunity should be made available to all members of the school community, not just those who have the most time and energy to devote.

6. *Collaboration with the community.* Schools can help families gain access to support services from other community agencies. Schools can also help mobilize families and other community groups in efforts to improve community life.

A comprehensive community-engagement program should include activities across all of the dimensions. These activities, on the face of them, seem to be primarily one way, from the school to the community. "Such a school-centric frame assumes that schools are the primary influences for learning in the lives of children and youth rather than one part of students' broader developmental contexts" (Honig, Kahne, & McLaughlin, 2001, p. 1001). Honig and colleagues argue that school and community connections must be constructed in terms of both their capacities for opportunities to learn and their opportunities to teach. Much traditional thinking underestimates the importance of the structures and activities outside of schools among the peer groups that provide learning communities of support for students.

When considering the focus of community engagement, school leaders can think about these connections in terms of opportunities to teach. Teachers can extend the space and time for teaching into the community, using the "access to funds of knowledge about their students' provided by connections with communities and families, the involvement of community partners in teaching who also provide resources connected to real world contexts, and the opportunities for teachers as well as students to create expanded professional networks and supports" (Honig et al., 2001,

p. 1017). Such engagement is likely also to result in a realignment of the ways in which schools view the funds of knowledge for teaching (Moll, Amanti, Neff, & Gonzalez, 1992) that are available to students in lower-income communities but are often undervalued by schools.

Data regarding both the nature and quality of parental, family, and community involvement in the school should be gathered as part of schoolwide data inquiry. Furthermore, research-based best practices should be part of the information gathered to support the goals of parent and family involvement in the school. These data can serve as the basis for collaborative problem solving with the community.

Culture and Climate for Student Learning

Together, parent and community involvement, professional learning communities, professional development, alignment of instruction to challenging, agreed-upon standards, and school mission and goals have the potential of developing a culture of continuous improvement. For decades researchers have pointed out the importance of school culture for educational effectiveness (see Bryk & Driscoll, 1988; Bryk et al., 1993; Coleman & Hoffer, 1987; Newmann et al., 1996; Purkey & Smith, 1983). The common standards, the communication among staff and between staff and community, the engagement on activities to support effective instruction and improved learning, and the many rituals in the schools and classrooms that happen every day provide a solid foundation for a culture of improvement. Such positive school cultures contribute to the school's capacity to successfully implement high-quality reform strategies and interventions (Berends, Kirby, Naftel, & McKelvey, 2001; Sebring & Bryk, 2000).

The early research on effective schools indicated that a safe and orderly climate is associated with academic success (Clark, Lotto, & McCarthy, 1980; Rutter et al., 1979). Research and program development by Crone and Horner (2003) and Charney and Wood (1981) have focused on schoolwide prosocial programs and their effects on both social behavior and academic outcomes. This work with schoolwide positive behavior support and schoolwide social curriculum like the Responsive Classroom (Charney, 1992) collectively indicates that schools that are supportive, responsive environments for students have better attendance, fewer office referrals, more academic engagement from students, and greater gain in achievement test results in comparison to schools without such programs (Elliott, 1993, 1997; Gresham, Sugai, Horner, Quinn, & McInerney, 1998).

The school community examines evidence as to how well the school's culture is supporting students' social development and the extent to which there is a safe climate for all students and adults. Data can help "develop a shared understanding of the problem(s) and to mobilize the school to respond wisely and vigorously" (Hawley & Sykes, 2007, p. 58).

Resources Aligned to Goals

Even the best principals with the best teachers with the most supportive parents and communities need additional resources to support their work. One of the challenges of states and districts has been to focus resources in a consistent, stable, and focused way to support a common purpose for teaching and learning (Berends, Bodilly, & Kirby, 2002; Bryk et al., 1998; Garet et al., 2001; Glennan, Bodilly, Galegher, & Kerr, 2004; Hawley, 2002; Murphy & Hallinger, 1992). Political leadership and support, along with regulatory and financial support, need to be in place for effective schools to sustain their improvement efforts (Bodilly & Berends, 1999).

Political and Leadership Support. To support schools in focusing resources on teaching and learning, the systemic support provided by states and districts includes such features as stability of leadership in the district and state offices; a perception that the instructional interventions and strategies in the schools are high priority and high quality; a lack of budget crisis (or some other crisis); a history of trust between the central offices and the schools; and respect for the professional autonomy of schools especially over curriculum and instruction, budgets, positions, and staffing. In their research on schoolwide improvement efforts focusing on teaching and learning, Bodilly and Berends (1999) found that school principals and teachers perceived that these factors were directly linked to greater efforts at implementing interventions focused on curriculum and instruction. When political leadership and support were missing, school respondents reported that their own efforts stalled or were less intense.

Regulatory and Financial Support. Although crucial, central office political support and attention must also be buttressed by significant changes in their regulatory and financial practices. School improvement focused on teaching and learning is about a school transforming and sustaining itself into an organization dedicated to facing and solving its particular problems and improving its students' educational opportunities and achievement. Such efforts are not confined to the adoption of simply a new curriculum or a few new instructional strategies.

Instead, it requires the rethinking of, reflecting on, and engaging in the various indicators of effective schooling discussed earlier. Such effective schooling cannot be cultivated without significant changes in resource allocation for instructional positions, materials, technology, professional development, and other items and activities. Thus some school-level issues, problems, and needs are likely to be facilitated if there is some local modicum of control over the curriculum and instruction, the budgets, the positions and staffing, and, most essentially, the school mission.

In short, the state- and district-level politics, policies, and practices could boost or derail the effort to promote effective teaching and learning. Schools look to district leadership, climate, and regulations to understand if it is worth their time and effort to invest in transforming. It is important to note that the barriers to innovations and transformation at the district may be increasing. Districts are facing new and building pressures to see the performance of their lowest-performing schools increase substantially. If districts react to this pressure with past routinized behaviors, they will seek to increase central control while applying it in the usual fragmentary fashion. Such policies significantly conflict with the effective school processes outlined here. This top-down approach, although possibly producing short-term gains, cannot provide the long-term capacity and capability building needed at the school level.

Data regarding the nature, type, and allocation of resources are central to data-based decision making and school-improvement processes. The allocation of all types of resources—political, human, and financial—must be aligned with goals and priorities set by the school. For example, leaders make sure that teachers have all the necessary materials and resources required to be highly effective instructors. They ask such questions as: Are the professional development dollars going to the teachers that need the most help in a certain subject area?

Data-Based Processes for Analyzing Programs and Practices Linked to School Improvement

Under NCLB, schools and their leaders are accountable for student performance. Adequate yearly progress is determined by measures on achievement tests. However, to chart and implement a plan to meet student achievement goals, leaders and their schools must engage in school improvement along the key components of effective schooling outlined in this chapter. School principals, teachers, and staff need to understand how well the school is progressing on a number of indicators or pathways. As such, school leaders need to focus on such questions as these: Are we aligning professional development with our student learning goals? In what areas is the school doing well? Parent involvement? In what areas does the school need to work? Professional learning communities? What information is needed to begin, continue, and sustain a path toward improvement? Relying on the use of a wider array of data, school leaders can begin to address these types of questions to support schools in their efforts to improve. In fact, successful school leaders use data extensively to guide schools in their decision making, goal setting, and progress monitoring.

Today, a number of opportunities exist for school leaders to thoughtfully use data to identify problems, define needs, set goals, plan interventions, and evaluate progress. In the chapters that follow, we outline some specific ways in which school leaders can collect data for school improvement and student learning by linking data to mission and goals, using data for school-improvement planning, compiling and gathering data, and involving the school community. Later in the book we focus on analyzing data. Specifically, we describe some key principles in measurement and assessment, how to analyze data and link it to the key indicators of effective schools. In the final sections of the text, we discuss using data to make decisions, including how to benchmark mission and goals, and set priorities for school improvement.

Although there is no one path toward school improvement (Fullan, 1999; Newmann, 2002; Newmann et al., 1996), school leaders can promote their school's focus on teaching and learning by using a wide array of data to enhance the schooling processes. This involves data collection, analysis, reflection, decision making, and continuous monitoring. It is the first step, data collection, to which we turn in the next few chapters, after we set out the steps in data-based decision making in the next chapter.

Discussion Questions

1. As discussed in the chapter, it is important for school leaders to anchor school-improvement efforts in a schoolwide focus on teaching and learning. This is done by attending to the school's mission and goals, rigorous content standards, curricular alignment, the professional community of teachers, the climate of the school, and the relationship between schools and communities. Describe one of these domains with which you are particularly proficient and one with which you currently struggle.

2. The chapter is organized around nine indicators of school improvement and provides insight regarding the utility of data in each of these domains. Choose two of these domains that are challenges in your school. Based on the insights provided in the chapter, create action steps for how you might go about collecting, analyzing, and using data to bring positive change to these challenging domains.

3. Based on your current experience as an educational leader, describe what comprises your existing data-collection efforts.

Section II

Collecting Data for School

Improvement and Student Learning

The Steps in Data-Based Decision Making

Linking Data to Mission and Goals

The mission and goals of a school play a pivotal role in guiding the curricular and programmatic activities of the school. As such, school leaders must continually engage data to set strategic goals that are consistent with the vision and mission of their school and address key school effectiveness indicators. This chapter provides key steps to understanding how to prioritize multiple types and sources of data to chart a path for achieving the school's mission. This alignment between data and the school's mission allows school leaders to continually monitor the progress toward reaching goals and aspirations.

VIGNETTE REVISITED

You have made a presentation to the leadership group of Rosemont School about the essential indicators of school effectiveness to guide a plan for school improvement that focuses on teaching and learning. Your presentation was a success. The council members seem to understand the key components of effective schooling and the interrelationships among multiple influences on student outcomes. They also appear to recognize that resources for

---

> school improvement should be focused on particular strategies for achieving high-priority goals for students. The leadership group wants to know what is next on the road to improvement.

Because the former principal had been at the school so long and was comfortable with the teachers, the students, and the parents, it seems that he led by intuition. You, however, are new to the role, the school, and the community. Moreover, given a new awareness of recent declines in student performance coupled with new demands by state and local policymakers for accountability, you recognize that you need a systematic way to understand the needs for improvement. In particular, the school needs to face the challenges of increasing student achievement for every student in the school. You suggest that if progress is to be made, the school needs a great deal more information than is now available about student learning and the efficacy of different approaches to improvement.

When confronted with the prospects of embarking on a school-improvement process, school principals usually ask such questions as these: Where should I start? How do I know if we are focusing on the *right* problem? How do I prioritize our initiatives? How will we know if we are making a difference?

These questions involve three key concepts: mission, benchmarking, and problem finding. Figure 3.1 portrays the process involving these three concepts. The first step involves the mission and evaluating it from a school-improvement perspective based on data-based decision making. The next step is to benchmark the mission, establishing important outcomes and processes critical to fulfilling the mission. The final step is defining the problem on which to focus school-improvement efforts. Each step is discussed in what follows. The chapter ends by elaborating on these steps in the data-based decision-making process describing specific activities school leaders use for effective school improvement.

Figure 3.1 The Process of Using Data to Strengthen Schools

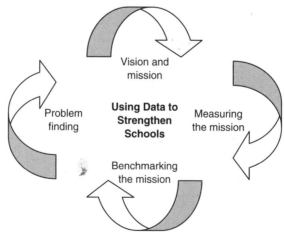

MISSION

Much has been written about the importance of a compelling mission for a school organization. A mission is the compass for the school; it provides a snapshot of what the school community values; it tells everyone what the school has set out to accomplish; and it sets the direction for where the school is headed. Mission statements respond to core questions such as the following: What are our key goals? Why do we exist? And what are we trying to accomplish?

Although educators bemoan the use or overuse of mission statements and often believe they are superficial statements tacked on to the schoolhouse walls, starting with a compelling mission statement can be a key first step to data-based decision making because it states exactly what the school will achieve. This statement provides the first step in the benchmarking process by articulating the specific areas of focus that should be measured to monitor progress and achievement.

Consider the mission statement of Rosemont School (see Figure 3.2). What do we learn about Rosemont School from the mission statement? We learn that the school values a school environment that is safe and nurturing and provides opportunities for all students to learn. We also learn what the school aspires to achieve, namely, that all students reach performance goals and act with respect and responsibility.

Figure 3.2 Rosemont School Mission

The mission of Rosemont School is to provide a safe and secure environment and provide opportunities for all students to perform at or above grade level in reading, writing, and mathematics while demonstrating responsibility and self-control.

An important first step in the data-based decision-making process is to evaluate your mission statement to ensure that it is not just the principal's mission statement or that of a select committee, but is truly embraced by the entire school community. This broad-based support is essential because the mission of a school can be the guidepost for school-improvement efforts. As such, the school community should review the mission statement regularly. This chapter provides insight to help school leaders with the task of continually monitoring a school's progress against its mission statement through a data-based decision-making processes. Figure 3.3 outlines potential ways for a school community to consider means of evaluating the efficacy of the mission statement.

Figure 3.3 Ways to Evaluate Your School Mission

Ways to evaluate your mission statement:

• Is your mission statement brief and to the point?

• Is your mission statement understandable and meaningful to your school's internal community (students, teachers, and parents)?

• Is your mission statement clear, understandable, and embraced by members of your school's external community (community leaders, outside agencies)?

• Does the mission statement clearly specify your school's reason for being? what student needs your school will meet? how the school will meet their needs?

• Is the statement specific enough to have a clear focus yet broad enough to allow flexibility in implementation?

• Does the statement serve as a rallying point, motivator, and a compass for the school?

• Is the mission statement measurable? Can you provide evidence that the mission can be fulfilled?

BENCHMARKING

The concept of benchmarking gained popularity with the advent of Total Quality Management (TQM). In 1993 an Industry Week (Benson, 1993, p. 48) article claimed, "In 10 short years, TQM has become as pervasive a part of business thinking as quarterly financial results." A foundation of TQM is benchmarking and measurement, which is operationalized by setting goals, evaluating performance, comparing performance to goals, and adapting accordingly (Juran, 1992; Powell, 1995). In education benchmarking is used to analyze performance, practices, and processes (Farmer & Taylor, 1997).

Benchmarking can serve three key purposes in the school-improvement process. First, benchmarks provide a baseline from which the effectiveness of programs and initiatives can be evaluated and monitored. For example, a school-improvement team at an elementary school has decided to focus on writing after a thorough investigation of the writing test scores, writing instruction, writing curriculum, and a close examination of student

writing assignments across teachers and grades in the school. As a result of this inquiry the school is embarking on a series of professional development workshops to address writing in all subjects and will develop writing rubrics that are aligned with district and state writing standards. The benchmarks that will be used as a baseline to evaluate progress in the writing initiatives will be the writing test scores and samples of student writing assignments before the implementation of the professional development programs.

Second, benchmarks can provide a measure for ongoing program development and improvement. To continually monitor changes in writing instruction, it is important to implement frequent, rigorous classroom assessments that are aligned with the content standards. These ongoing assessments, often termed *formative assessments*, can provide feedback about student learning within the context of a curricular unit. In this way benchmarking plays a pivotal role in the process of continuous improvement.

Third, benchmarks can be used to make decisions regarding the allocation of human, material, and financial resources. Continuing with our example of enhancing writing instruction, as we continue to benchmark change, it is possible to see that the students in one teacher's class may need additional assistance; therefore, for example, a writing specialist can be assigned to that class along with two student teachers to reduce class size so that smaller group instruction can take place.

Benchmarking the Mission: Outcomes

A solid first step in the process of data-based decision making involves establishing benchmarks that correspond to the key components of your mission statement. Using the key concepts in your mission statement as the first step in benchmarking can help answer the question, "With so much potential data, where do I start?" Figure 3.4 provides an example of the benchmarking process. Returning to our example of Rosemont School, we can determine through its mission statement a number of school goals, including the following two specific goals:

1. Provide a safe and secure environment

2. Teach all students to perform at or above grade level in reading, writing, and mathematics

Starting with these two goals, we first must ask, how is Rosemont School currently doing? To answer this question we need to benchmark the current performance of Rosemont School on these goals. Only after we know how Rosemont School is doing in regard to these goals does it make sense to begin to embark on any discussion of school change or reform.

Using the Outcome Data Collection Planning Guide in Figure 3.4, we can see that two primary guiding questions are the following: Do students, parents, and teachers feel that Rosemont School is safe and secure? Are all students performing at or above grade level in reading, writing, and mathematics? Once we have established what we want to learn from the data, we next need to determine if we have existing school data to answer these questions. In some instances we have sufficient data to begin to answer the questions, and in other cases we need additional data to complete the benchmarking picture of the school outcomes. In the case of Rosemont School, as outlined in Figure 3.4, there is enough available data to begin benchmarking the mission.

Figure 3.4 Outcome Data Collection Planning Guide

Content areas for which data is needed	What we want to learn from the data	Data we have at school from reports and other sources	Data we need to collect	Sources of new data	Who should be involved in data collection
Safe and secure environment	Do parents, teachers, and students feel school is safe and nurturing?	Number of discipline infractions, office referrals, suspensions Results from annual district parent survey	Input from students	Student focus groups	Student council, homeroom teachers
Perform at or above grade level in reading	Are all students meeting performance goals in reading?	End-of-year standardized tests; course grades; formative assessments	Level of reading in content areas, usage of library	Assignments in science and social studies; books checked out from library; accelerated reading	Librarian, team of teachers

Benchmarking School Processes

One of the primary responsibilities of school leaders is to help people confront problems. The way you confront problems is to identify them, and one way you identify problems is by looking at data. As educational leaders collect and analyze school data, they are in a position to serve as problem solvers for the school community. In fact, most school principals will say they solve problems all day—students are waiting in the office for disciplinary action, teachers are absent due to the flu and substitutes are needed, parents are calling to complain about the algebra teacher because a high number of students are failing, and on and on. Early studies of the principalship confirm that school leaders are rapid problem solvers (McPherson, Crowson, & Pitner, 1986).

PROBLEM FINDING

The work of school improvement, however, requires a much more focused, stable, and long-term approach. The first step in this process is problem finding, or defining the problem. Imagine you get the school report card for Rosemont School and you see that you did not meet adequate yearly progress in reading and writing. What is the problem? Is there only one main problem or are there several? Are the teachers not implementing the curriculum? If so, the solution would be professional development. Are students frequently sent out of the class for disciplinary action? That problem would lead to a different solution. Are some students meeting benchmarks while others are not? If groups of students are not meeting performance standards, the solution may be to have targeted small-group instruction. These examples suggest that how the problem is defined is a crucial first step. Schools can spend much time, energy, and resources addressing the wrong problem or a problem that will not actually impact the result you are trying to address. Therefore, problem finding is a first step in problem solving. And the importance of data? Without data, it is very difficult to find the problem.

Imagine the following scenario from the benchmarking process of Rosemont School: The data analysis has revealed that many Latino parents do not feel welcome at school and do not regularly attend parent-teacher conferences. Furthermore, their children often come to school late and miss some of first period. First period is schoolwide reading. In addition, there is a persistent achievement gap in the school between majority white students and students of color. The gap is stable across the past three years. The largest gap is in reading and writing. Students are often assigned to bring books home from the library and read with their parents.

It is clear that describing the situation is only the first step. Before the Rosemont School community can solve the problem, they first must identify it. "Problem finding is the act of transforming an uncomfortable or irritating situation in a question which can be answered, or into a hypothesis which can be tested. Problem finding is the first and most crucial element of problem solving" (McPherson, Crowson, & Pitner, 1986, p. 273). Some problems are already clearly presented. In this case the problem is well defined and thought can already be turned to problem solving. The problem of finding substitute teachers is a presented problem; it makes sense to proceed to finding solutions. However, data-based decision making is usually aimed at discovering problems—problems that are not yet defined—where problem-finding is the first step (McPherson et al., 1986, p. 277).

Steps in the Process of Using Data to Strengthen Schools

How do you go about discovering problems in your school? In the chapters that follow, we will walk though the various steps involved, as portrayed in Figure 3.5. As mentioned earlier in this chapter, the fist step is to evaluate the mission statement. The next step is collecting data to link to the mission. The third step is compiling the data for benchmarking the outcomes and processes, which may involve standardized achievement scores, formative assessments, and other data used for measuring the pathways to school improvement. Fourth, school leaders involve the school community to analyze the data to identify a problem in their school. A variety of analyses across several school years, by grade level by different groups of students, by teacher within grade level is helpful for understanding the specificity and magnitude of the problem. These analyses involve what we call "peeling the onion" to examine various layers of data—to peel them in ways that allow for getting deep into the data for understanding potential problems and possibilities. Identifying the key problem is important for focusing school-improvement efforts.

We discuss the details of these steps and the process of using data in the chapters that follow. The next section addresses the collection of data for school improvement and student learning, describing in depth various standardized achievement scores (Chapter 4), using formative assessments (Chapter 5), and measuring the various pathways to successful schools (Chapter 6). Then, in section III, we describe the activities involved in analyzing data by involving the school community (Chapter 7) and by doing a variety of descriptive analyses of different data to identify the school problem (Chapter 8). In the concluding section of the book, we discuss evidence-based decision making and setting priorities for school improvement (Chapter 9). Chapter 10 provides a summary of the book and emphasizes that the process of leading with data is a continuous discovery process.

Figure 3.5 Steps in the Process of Using Data to Strengthen Schools

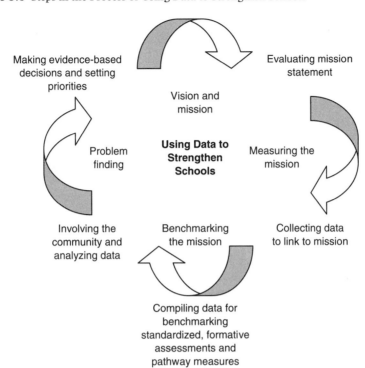

Discussion Questions

1. Evaluate the mission statement for your school using the questions in Figure 3.3.

2. Fill out the Outcome Data Collection Planning Guide for your school.

3. What problem areas do you anticipate after reviewing your mission statement?

Using Standardized Achievement Data for School-Improvement Planning

Measuring Achievement Outcomes

One of the key sources of data for school-improvement planning is standardized achievement tests. Within the current policy environment, schools, principals, and teachers are held accountable for student learning as measured by standardized assessments. At the end of this chapter, you will have a deeper understanding of standardized achievement tests and how they can be used to help identify strengths and weaknesses.

VIGNETTE REVISITED

The leadership team at Rosemont School is energized around the planning that has aligned mission and goals to school-improvement processes and specific outcomes. The team members, however, are a bit overwhelmed by all the possible types and sources of data that can be used for data-based decision making. They would like a guide that could help them sort out

---

the different types of data and their uses so they can begin to decide what data they will use and who can help them collect data that is not yet available. The team decided to start by acquiring a deeper understanding of the standardized achievement test data for their school while also gathering other types of data that measure student achievement and learning outcomes. The team knows that these standardized test data are the basis for NCLB accountability and the school's published report card, indicating all the subgroups that have and have not met adequate yearly progress.

Standardized achievement tests are one of the main elements of both school-improvement planning and data-based decision making. Over the past decade, schools have increasingly been held accountable for student learning as measured by standardized achievement tests because of No Child Left Behind. Standardized achievement tests are the basis for determining if Rosemont School meets adequate yearly progress each year. Standardized achievement tests, which are typically administered at the end of a school year, are considered a type of summative evaluation or measure. Summative tests are used to assess how well the student has mastered the material; thus they provide summary information about the student. What makes a test a *standardized* achievement test? One main feature of a standardized achievement test is comparison data in the form of *norms*. Norms are a set of test scores based on the test results of an external group or standardization group that takes the test to provide comparative data. The norm group helps provide a *relative* interpretation of the test information. National norms are based on students sampled from across the country, whereas state or local norms compare students from a specific locale. For achievement test results, norms are typically reported by age and grade level.

Standardized achievement tests are also constructed through an elaborate process of item-writing and item-testing before the test is finalized. A group of educators and test developers will review curriculum, standards, and textbooks throughout the nation (or the state if they are writing a standardized test for one state) to align the test questions and items to standards and the curriculum. Items are drafted based on content outlines aligned with the standards and curriculum. The fist step in the test development is to use the items with a group of students, not to measure the students' achievement but to ascertain information or properties about the items themselves: Are the items clear and unambiguous? Is there only one correct answer? Is the item too difficult for the grade level? A bank of test items is developed for each content domain (e.g., reading, mathematics) and standard instructions for test administration are developed.

Once standardized tests are developed, it is important to assess their validity and reliability. *Validity* refers to the extent to which a test measures what it is intended to measure. For example, if a standardized achievement test is supposed to test vocabulary in a valid manner, we need to assess whether the set of items really are a test of vocabulary. Perhaps they are not because the items are more a test of spelling or reading comprehension. In general, the key validity questions pertaining to standardized achievement tests relate to either content validity or criterion validity. Content validity asks, does the test content reflect the standards, curriculum, and level of material that is supposed to be taught to the specific grade level tested? A criterion validity question is, does a student who is exposed to the content and material covered on the test do better than a student not exposed or not taught does?

Reliability refers to the extent to which the test measure is accurate—meaning that the test is consistent each time it is administered and each time it is used. In other words, if a test is reliable, a change in a student's score can be attributed to the student, meaning the student has actually learned more, rather than to an unreliable test that has many ambiguous items or items that are susceptible to guessing. Standardized achievement tests tend to have high reliability because of the extensive checking and revising of items before they make their way into the final test version.

UNDERSTANDING STANDARDIZED ACHIEVEMENT TEST DATA

There are two main types of standardized achievements test data: criterion-referenced and norm-referenced tests. A *criterion-referenced test* indicates the percentage of students who master content-specific objectives. As such, a criterion-referenced test focuses on mastery of the skills, or criteria, being tested. Criterion-referenced tests differ from *norm-referenced tests* in that the focus of criterion-referenced tests is on assessing the performance of an individual as measured against a standard, or criterion, such as a specific skill. Norm-referenced tests assess achievement against the performance of others who take the same test, which is the norm group.

Criterion-Referenced Tests

Table 4.1 provides an example of schoolwide achievement test results that focus on students' mastery of specific learning objectives. As such, it serves as an example of data from a criterion-referenced achievement test. The data in Table 4.1 are reported for Grades 3, 4, and 5. The columns on the left report the content area and content-specific objectives, or the criteria that were tested for each grade level. The data presented in this table are the percentage of students in each grade level who have mastered the content-specific objectives or criteria. In third grade, for example, 44 percent of the students mastered Reading Objective 2, or Basic Understanding. In Math Computation, 82 percent of the third graders mastered Objective 43, Add Whole Numbers. You may notice that not all criteria, or objectives, are tested in every year and, therefore, in each of the grade levels several measurements are left blank. The blanks show that the students in this grade level were not tested for the specific objective. In third grade, for example, the students were not tested for Oral Comprehension, which is Reading Objective 1. The third graders were not tested for the Math Computation Objectives 48 through 51 either.

Table 4.1 Criterion-Reference Achievement Test

		Grade		
Test Area	Objective	3	4	5
Reading	01 Oral Comprehension	–	–	–
	02 Basic Understanding	44	58	69
	03 Analyze Text	35	37	70
	04 Evaluate and Extend Meaning	49	63	42
	05 Identify Reading Strategies	41	43	41
Language	06 Introduction to Print	–	–	–
	07 Sentence Structure	54	26	50
	08 Writing Strategies	39	30	37
	09 Editing Skills	34	49	57
Mathematics	10 Number and Number Relations	62	58	25
	11 Computation and Numerical Estimation	49	37	37
	12 Operation Concepts	79	58	55
	13 Measurement	75	25	20
	14 Geometry and Spatial Sense	51	75	20
	15 Data Analysis, Stats, and Probability	40	44	25
	16 Patterns, Functions, Algebra	37	58	32
	17 Problem Solving and Reasoning	29	36	50
Science	18 Word Problems	–	–	42
	19 Science Inquiry	45	36	38
	20 Physical Science	20	10	7
	21 Life Science	41	20	25
	22 Earth and Space Science	21	15	11
	23 Science and Technology	66	49	14
	24 Personal and Social Perspectives	73	33	39
	25 History and Nature of Science	—	–	–
Social Studies	26 Geographical Perspectives	52	36	26
	27 Historical and Cultural Perspectives	47	37	17
	28 Civics and Government Perspectives	44	30	30
	29 Economic Perspectives	55	33	34

Test Area	Objective	Grade		
		3	4	5
Word Analysis	30 Consonants (Word Analysis)	92	–	–
	31 Sight Words	–	–	–
	32 Vowels (Word Analysis)	29	–	–
	33 Contractions and Compounds	–	–	–
	34 Roots and Affixes	27	–	–
Vocab	35 Word Meaning	37	37	37
	36 Multimeaning Words	17	36	79
	37 Words in Context	70	15	21
Lang Mech	38 Sentences, Phrases, Clauses	72	37	30
	39 Writing Conventions	38	55	64
Spelling	40 Vowels (Spelling)	41	32	21
	41 Consonants (Spelling)	52	53	6
	42 Structural Units	65	10	8
Math Computation	43 Add Whole Numbers	82	–	–
	44 Subtract Whole Numbers	64	–	–
	45 Multiply Whole Numbers	53	42	36
	46 Divide Whole Numbers	19	27	23
	47 Decimals	64	60	17
	48 Fractions	–	–	8
	49 Integers	–	–	–
	50 Percents	–	–	–
	51 Order of Operations	–	–	–

SOURCE: Paul Changas.

As evidenced in Table 4.1, although students in each grade are given a grade-level-specific test, we can still look at particular objectives across grade levels to compare the percentage of students who master each objective. On Vocabulary Objective 36, or Multimeaning Words, the percentage of students in the school who master the objective increases from third to fifth grade. Specifically, the percentage of students increases from 17 percent in third grade to 36 percent in fourth grade and finally to 79 percent in fifth grade. On the other hand, there are several objectives in which the percentage of students who master the objective decreases across the grade levels. For example, on the Vocabulary Objective 37, Words in Context, the percentage of students who master the objective decreases from 70 percent in third grade to 15 percent in fourth and 21 percent in fifth. On the Mathematics Objective 13, Measurement, the percentage of students who master the objective also decreases from 75 percent in third grade to 25 percent in fourth and 20 percent in fifth. These are examples of content areas in which principals and teachers should focus their efforts. It is important to remember that when comparing across grades you are not comparing the same groups of students but totally different groups of students because the table presents data from only one year.

Criterion- and Norm-Referenced Test Data Disaggregated by Teacher

The data in Table 4.2 will allow us to compare the overall performance of the fifth graders at a particular school to a national reference group of fifth graders. As such, this table provides an example of test data that is norm referenced. Additionally, the data provided in Table 4.2 is disaggregated by grade level and will thus allow for a comparison of the performance of the three fifth-grade classes at the same school. Notice that the left column of this table contains the same Language Arts and Mathematics content areas and objectives, or criteria, tested in fifth grade that we discussed when looking at the schoolwide data. In this regard Table 4.2 does provide criterion-referenced data, yet it provides an additional comparison group of scores for a nationally normed group of fifth-grade students.

Table 4.2 Disaggregated Criterion- and Norm-Referenced Data

Objectives Performance by School/Teacher Grade 5		Percentage of Students Mastering Each Objective			Teacher			Average Objectives Performance Index (OPI)			Teacher		
Objectives Performance Index (OPI)*		Total School	National*	Difference	Jones	Robinson	Smith	Total School	National*	Difference	Jones	Robinson	Smith
	Reading												
02	Basic Understanding	69	54	+15	86	59	58	● 78	■ 73	+5	● 87	■ 73	■ 74
03	Analyze Text	70	54	+16	55	55	65	● 79	■ 72	+7	● 85	■ 73	● 76
04	Evaluate/Extend Meaning	42	35	+7	27	27	31	■ 67	■ 62	+5	● 77	■ 61	■ 65
05	Identify Reading Strategies	41	33	+8	23	23	31	■ 66	■ 62	+4	● 77	■ 60	■ 63
	Vocabulary												
35	Word Meaning	37	29	+8	46	27	35	■ 63	■ 60	+3	■ 69	■ 58	■ 62
36	Multimeaning Words	79	71	+8	89	68	77	● 83	● 80	+3	● 87	● 80	● 84
37	Words in Context	21	16	+5	25	14	23	■ 53	○ 49	+4	■ 58	○ 49	■ 53
	Language												
07	Sentence Structure	50	40	+10	68	55	27	■ 68	■ 66	+2	● 76	■ 68	■ 62
08	Writing Strategies	37	29	+8	54	32	23	● 65	■ 65	+3	■ 72	■ 64	■ 61
09	Editing Skills	57	55	+2	75	64	31	■ 73	■ 73	00	● 81	● 76	■ 63

	Language Mechanics												
38	Sentence, Phrases, Clauses	30	33	-3	46	32	12	■ 61	■ 63	-2	■ 70	■ 61	■ 56
39	Conventions	64	64	0	82	59	50	● 77	● 76	+1	● 82	● 76	■ 71
	Mathematics												
10	Number and Number Relations	25	29	-4	43	23	8	■ 57	■ 59	-2	■ 68	■ 50	■ 53
11	Computation and Estimation	37	36	+1	54	45	12	■ 65	■ 66	-1	■ 73	■ 64	■ 59
12	Operation Concepts	55	61	-6	71	45	46	■ 72	● 75	-3	● 83	■ 65	■ 69
13	Measurement	20	27	-7	36	14	8	■ 59	■ 61	-2	■ 68	■ 55	■ 56
14	Geometry and Spatial Sense	20	27	-7	39	14	4	■ 57	■ 60	-3	■ 68	■ 52	■ 52
15	Data, Statistics, and Probability	25	28	-3	43	23	8	■ 61	■ 62	-1	■ 70	■ 57	■ 56
16	Patterns, Functions, Algebra	32	32	0	50	32	12	■ 64	■ 63	+1	■ 71	■ 60	■ 56
17	Problem Solving and Reasoning	50	50	0	75	36	35	■ 67	■ 69	-2	● 79	■ 59	■ 64
	Math Computation												
45	Multiply Whole Numbers	36	40	-4	61	36	8	■ 55	■ 62	-7	■ 70	■ 56	○ 41
46	Divide Whole Numbers	23	28	-5	39	14	12	■ 52	■ 57	-5	■ 64	■ 51	○ 40
47	Decimals	17	21	-4	39	9	0	■ 57	■ 61	-4	■ 68	■ 56	○ 46
48	Fractions	8	6	+2	18	5	0	○ 35	○ 36	-1	○ 45	○ 32	○ 27
	Number of Students:	76	-	-	28	22	26	76	-	-	28	22	26

SOURCE: Paul Changas.

*OPI is the estimated number of items correct out of 100 had there been 100 items for that objective

● Mastery   (Range: 75–100 correct)

■ Partial Mastery   (Range: 50–74 correct)

○ Nonmastery   (Range: 0–49 correct)

* National Reference   Group Grade 5

Let's first focus our attention on the portion of the table labeled "Percentage of Students Mastering Each Objective." The first three columns allow us to make comparisons among the fifth graders at the school with the national reference group of fifth graders. Notice that the data in the column labeled "Total School" are the same percentages of students who mastered the content objectives that we saw in the table of school-wide data. The percentages in the second column are from the national reference group of fifth graders. The third column provides the differences between the fifth grade at the school and the national reference group. In the Reading, Vocabulary, and Language content areas, the fifth graders at the school clearly perform better than the national reference group. In particular, on the Reading Objectives 2 and 3, the school has 15 percent and 16 percent more students mastering the objectives, respectively. However, in the Language Mechanics, Mathematics, and Math Computation content areas, the fifth graders are achieving around the same percentage or less than the national reference group. For example, on the Mathematics Objectives 13 and 14, the percentage of students in the school is 7 percentage points below the national average. From the first three columns, it appears that the school may need to focus on the Language Mechanics, Mathematics, and Math Computation content areas in fifth grade.

We can also look at data disaggregated by classroom level to gain a deeper understanding of the performance of fifth graders at the school. Jones, Robinson, and Smith are the fifth-grade teachers at the school. Let's take a look at the percentage of students mastering each objective in each of the classes. From the data, it is evident that there is a higher percentage of students mastering the objectives in Jones's class than in Robinson's or Smith's classes. Furthermore, there is a higher percentage of students in Jones's class who are mastering the objectives than there is in both the school and national averages. If we compare Robinson's and Smith's classes, we see that there is a higher percentage of students mastering the Reading and Vocabulary content areas in Smith's class than in Robinson's. However, a higher percentage of students in Robinson's class than in Smith's class masters the Language, Language Mechanics, Mathematics, and Math Computation content areas. Notice that none of the students in Smith's class masters Decimals or Fractions. From this data analysis, it is clear that Smith's class in particular needs support. There could be opportunities for the teachers to work together to mentor and coach one another in areas of strength.

Let's now move on to the second portion of the table labeled "Average Objectives Performance Index (OPI)" to explore another method of examining student performance data on the same content objectives. The data in this section of the table are presented as Objectives Performance Index, or OPI, numbers. An OPI is an estimate of the number of items correct out of 100 had there been 100 items for that objective. In other words, an OPI is a fancy name for the percentage of items answered correctly for each objective. For example, let's say there were 15 items on the test for Math Computation Objective 45, or Multiply Whole Numbers. The reported Total School OPI is 55, which said that on average the fifth graders at the school answered 55 out of 100 items correctly. However, on the test the fifth graders answered 8.25 out of 15 items correctly, or 55 percent of the 15 items. We can use the OPI numbers to determine mastery levels.

In the upper left corner of the table you can see the three mastery levels and the OPI ranges. An OPI score between 75 and 100 is the Mastery level, represented by a filled in circle. An OPI score between 50 and 74 is Partial Mastery, represented by a partially filled square. And an OPI score between 0 and 49 is Nonmastery, represented by an unfilled circle.

With these data we can again compare the fifth graders at the school to the national reference group of fifth graders. Overall, the fifth graders at the school achieve Mastery or Partial Mastery in all of the objectives except for Fractions. Notice that the pattern of differences between the school and the national reference group are the same as when we used data on the percentage of students mastering each objective. The fifth graders at the school perform better than the national average in the Reading, Vocabulary, and Language content areas. And the fifth graders at the school perform at the same level or lower than the national average in Language Mechanics, Mathematics, and Math Computation content areas. Remember that we identified these same content areas as in need of assistance when we examined the percentage of students mastering the objectives.

If we look at the mastery levels of the three fifth-grade teachers, we see that Jones's students achieve Mastery on ten of the content objectives and achieve Partial Mastery on thirteen objectives. By comparison, Robinson's students achieve Mastery on three objectives and Smith's students achieve Mastery on only two objectives. All of the classes achieve Nonmastery on Fractions. Robinson's students also perform at the Nonmastery level on Words in Context. Notice that Smith's students perform at the Nonmastery level on all of the Math Computation objectives.

Even though Jones's class has the highest performance levels, there is still room for improvement. The students in Jones's class have mastered only two out of the twelve Mathematics objectives. Because each teacher needs to focus on Mathematics, the school may want to develop professional development specific to fifth-grade content objectives that improve curriculum, materials, and instructional strategies.

In addition, it is important to note that these data do not tell us anything about where the students in each classroom started at the beginning of the school year in terms of their achievement and proficiency. In other words, students in the various classrooms could be very different from each other, especially if the school implements grouping or tracking. Smith may be a better teacher but has students who start from a different level. The process of problem finding is imperative, as noted in Chapter 3. Collaborative teams come together to ask questions about the trends in the data and uncover information about competing hypotheses (such as high- achieving students are placed in a certain teacher's class). Then the discussion can narrow and focus on the question, what factors are impeding learning? Multiple sources of data are part of the deliberations, including data on the indicators and pathways to school improvement.

The question remains, how did Smith contribute to the students' achievement? Value-added assessment focuses on *gains* in academic achievement in a given year rather than a report of the students' *level* of achievement, or overall achievement score on a test, at one point (as depicted in the previous discussion and figures). Value added to student achievement measures the improvement in student performance from year to year (American Educational Research Association, 2004). "Students with low starting scores can show strong gains and vice versa. In this way, value-added assessments allow us to see how educators add to student knowledge, over and above what students' families and neighborhoods contribute" (AERA, p. 1). The benefit of using value-added assessments is that data-based decision making is focused on gains in achievement, and statistically the playing field is leveled when comparing different populations of students by "removing the substantial differences in student background" (AERA, p. 4). In short, "value-added assessment is an improvement over simply comparing end-of-year achievement scores without controlling for what students knew at the beginning of the year" (AERA, p. 4).

The importance of value-added measurement is growing as some states are now using value-added accountability approaches to measure Yearly Academic Progress under the provisions of No Child Left Behind.

The Variety of Norm-Referenced Test Scores

Multiple scores are used to report standardized achievement results relative to the norm group. Table 4.3 presents a norm-referenced report for one fifth-grade student. Norm-referenced results are beneficial for educators because they allow us to understand student performance relative to other fifth graders. Notice that the content areas Mathematics and Math Computation are in the left column, along with Math Composite, which is the student's overall performance in math. There are four types of norm-referenced test scores on this report. They are National Stanine, Normal Curve Equivalent, Scale Score, and National Percentile.

National Stanines are normalized standard scores that divide the normal curve into broad intervals ranging from one to nine. We can interpret the stanines ranging between one and three as Below Average, between four and six as Average, and between seven and nine as Above Average. National Stanines lack precision because we are not able to determine if a score is at the top or the bottom of the stanine. With stanines we are also unable to observe small changes in performance. Notice that the student

Table 4.3 Student Norm-Referenced Achievement Data

Student:			Teacher:	Smith
Grade:	05		School:	
Birth date:			System:	
ID:	0000000001		Test Date:	

Norm-Referenced Subtest/Composite	National Stanine	Normal Curve Equivalent	Scale Score	National Percentile
Mathematics	5	46	640	42
Math Computation	6	61	657	70
Math Composite	5	53	649	56

SOURCE: Paul Changas.

in this report has National Stanines of 5 on Mathematics, 6 on Math Computation, and 5 on Math Composite. From the data, it is clear that this student falls into the Average range of National Stanines.

The next norm-referenced test score is the *Normal Curve Equivalent*, or NCE. NCE scores are normalized standard scores on an equal-interval scale. Similar to percentile ranks, NCE scores range from 1 to 99. However, unlike percentiles, a one-point interval change in an NCE score has the same meaning throughout the scale. NCE scores also have the same meaning across subtests. For example, the student in this report has a Mathematics NCE of 46, a Math Computation NCE of 61, and a Math Composite NCE of 53. This student performed better in Math Computation, and overall the student scored in the average range.

The third norm-referenced test score is the *Scale Score*. Scale Scores are created by mathematically transforming the student's raw score. Scale Score ranges depend on the particular test taken. For example, the test this student took has scale scores that range from 1 to 999. The Scale Scores span across all levels and grades of the test, which allows educators to measure the growth of the student from year to year. The student report indicates that this student has a Mathematics Scale Score of 640, a Math Computation Scale Score of 657, and a Math Composite Scale Score of 649. To interpret these scores, we would need either the student's scores from previous years or the normal distribution of other students' scores to make comparisons.

The final norm-referenced test score is the *National Percentile*. National Percentiles range from 1 to 99 and specify the percentage of students in a national norm group whose scores fall below the given student's test score. For example, the student in this report is at the 42nd percentile ranking for Mathematics, which means that he scored higher than 42 percent of the national scores. The student is at the 70th percentile ranking for Math

Computation and at the 56th percentile ranking for Math Composite. The intervals of national percentiles are unequal, which means that the score is a relative standing, but it changes from year to year based on the norm group taking the test.

Based on all of these interpretation methods, it should be clear that the results are consistent with one another. Each of the achievement test results shows that the student is in an average range. The norm-referenced results allow us to compare the student to national averages, and if we had the student's previous test results, we would be able to examine the student's performance over time.

Norm-Referenced Achievement Data by National Quartiles and Grade

Often norm-referenced data are reported according to national quartiles, as presented in Tables 4.4 and 4.5. These tables allow us to examine the percentage of students in the school who achieve in each of the four national quartiles: 1 percent to 25 percent, 26 percent to 50 percent, 51 percent to 75 percent, and 76 percent to 99 percent. When examining data in quartiles we would like to see a higher percentage of students achieving in the top two quartiles as opposed to the bottom two quartiles. In our analysis we will look for content areas where students are not evenly distributed among the quartiles to determine whether the school is excelling or falling short in that content area. The objective is to propel as many students as possible toward the third and fourth quartiles.

Let's now take a look at the schoolwide data for Grades 3, 4, and 5. The following table is broken down by the national quartiles for each grade level and the test content areas. You may notice that in addition to the content areas, Reading Composite, Language Composite, Math Composite, and Total Score categories have been included in the table. These categories have been added to enhance our overall understanding of the schoolwide data by combining similar content areas. For example, the Reading Composite is the overall score for the Reading and Vocabulary content areas.

In Grades 3 and 4, the percentage of students who achieve in each of the national quartiles is generally evenly distributed. However, in several content areas, the percentage of students is skewed either toward the top quartiles or the bottom quartiles. These are the content areas that we will examine closely. For example, in third grade, the Language Mechanics, Language Composite, and Spelling content areas are skewed toward the top quarter. In these content areas, there is a higher percentage of third graders performing in the top quarter. On the other hand, Reading

Composite and Science are content areas in which the percentage of third graders is skewed toward the bottom quarter. These content areas may need the most assistance in third grade.

Table 4.4 Percentage of Students by National Quartile and Grade for Reading and Math

Grade	Nat.	QTL	Read	Voc	Read. Comp.	Lang.	Lang. Mech.	Lang. Comp.	Math	Math Compu.	Math Comp.	Total Score
03	NP	76–99	19%	16%	19%	19%	31%	28%	22%	24%	23%	23%
	NP	51–75	24%	28%	26%	28%	25%	25%	24%	22%	23%	29%
	NP	26–50	29%	29%	29%	28%	24%	25%	28%	26%	27%	26%
	NP	01–25	28%	27%	27%	25%	21%	22%	26%	28%	25%	22%
04	NP	76–99	18%	20%	19%	19%	27%	25%	18%	24%	23%	22%
	NP	51–75	24%	23%	24%	25%	27%	24%	24%	26%	24%	28%
	NP	26–50	32%	33%	33%	30%	26%	27%	29%	30%	29%	29%
	NP	01–25	26%	24%	24%	26%	20%	24%	29%	20%	24%	21%
05	NP	76–99	21%	17%	20%	18%	17%	18%	11%	16%	15%	17%
	NP	51–75	22%	20%	22%	26%	21%	23%	21%	22%	21%	23%
	NP	26–50	29%	25%	25%	29%	33%	29%	34%	31%	29%	32%
	NP	01–25	28%	37%	33%	27%	28%	30%	33%	31%	35%	29%

SOURCE: Paul Changas.

Table 4.5 Percentage of Students by National Quartile and Grade for Science, Social Studies, Spelling, and Word Analysis

Grade	Nat.	QTL	Science	Soc. Studies	Spelling	Word Analysis
03	NP	76–99	19%	16%	31%	21%
	NP	51–75	16%	26%	23%	28%
	NP	26–50	27%	31%	21%	27%
	NP	01–25	38%	27%	25%	25%
04	NP	76–99	18%	21%	30%	–
	NP	51–75	21%	26%	25%	–
	NP	26–50	29%	27%	25%	–
	NP	01–25	33%	26%	19%	–
05	NP	76–99	14%	14%	22%	–
	NP	51–75	21%	20%	27%	–
	NP	26–50	32%	32%	26%	–
	NP	01–25	34%	35%	25%	–

SOURCE: Paul Changas.

As noted in Tables 4.4 and 4.5, the percentage of fifth-grade students achieving in each of the National Quartiles is less evenly distributed. In fact, in every content area except Spelling, higher percentages of students perform in the bottom quartiles than in the top quartiles. For example, in Mathematics, only 11 percent of the fifth graders performed in the top quarter, whereas 33 percent performed in the bottom quarter. This data should prompt the administrators in the school to focus their efforts on the fifth grade.

Now that we have analyzed schoolwide data by both the percentage of students mastering content area objectives and the distribution of students by National Quartiles, you may be interested in disaggregating the data further. Because we identified the fifth grade as a particular area of concern in this school, let's dig deeper by comparing classroom performance across this grade level.

Using Standardized Test Scores to Monitor Proficiency Levels

With the federal law No Child Left Behind, states are required to annually test every student in reading and mathematics in Grades 3–8. In this section we will look at data from one state's testing and accountability program to ascertain the extent to which schools are making adequate progress in meeting their accountability goals.

We will examine the state's testing data in reading for Grades 3–5 in an elementary school in Table 4.6. The standardized tests report student performance according to four achievement levels. Each achievement level is associated with a range of scale scores on the test. The number of questions that a student answered correctly is called a *raw score*. The raw scores are converted into a *scale score*, which allows for a comparison of the students' end-of-grade scores in a subject from one grade to the next. Students' scale scores are expected to go up each year as they progress through school. For Grades 3–5 the scale scores for reading range from 115 to 178, and for mathematics they range from 218 to 295. The state converts these scale score ranges into four different achievement levels.

Achievement levels serve as benchmarks. Recall that benchmarks serve as a *baseline* from which the effectiveness of programs and initiative can be evaluated and monitored. They also provide a measure for *ongoing* monitoring. And benchmarks provide information with which to make decisions regarding the allocation of human, material, and financial resources.

Achievement Levels. Achievement levels are performance standards that allow a student's performance to be compared to grade-level expectations. The judgment of many teachers is used to set the achievement levels. Four achievement levels (I, II, III, and IV) are reported in each subject area. The description of each achievement level follows:

Level I: Students performing at this level do not have sufficient mastery of knowledge and skills in the subject area to be successful at the next grade level. For example, the Level I scale score range for fourth-grade mathematics in Year 1 (for example, 2006–07) was 221–239.

Level II: Students performing at this level demonstrate inconsistent mastery of knowledge and skills in the subject area and are minimally prepared to be successful at the next grade level. For example, the Level II scale score range for fourth-grade mathematics in Year 2 (for example, 2007–08) as 240–246.

Level III: Students performing at this level consistently demonstrate mastery of the grade-level subject matter and skills and are well prepared for the next grade level. For example, the Level III scale score range for fourth-grade mathematics in Year 2 was 247–257.

Level IV: Students performing at this level consistently perform in a superior manner clearly beyond that required to be proficient at grade-level work. For example, the Level IV scale score range for fourth-grade mathematics in Year 2 was 258–285.

Students who perform at achievement Level III or Level IV are considered to be at grade-level proficiency or beyond in the content areas as determined by the state's accountability framework. These students demonstrate adequate preparation for the next grade level. It is important to note that districts or states may change the range of scale scores that correspond to each achievement level from year to year.

The data presented in Table 4.6 is for Grades 3, 4, and 5 over three academic school years. The data presented are the percentages of students in each grade level who have performed at Level III or IV on the end-of-grade tests in reading. Notice that the percentages are reported at the school level as well as at the district level. This allows you to compare the students at Rosemont to the average students in the district.

Table 4.6 Proficiency Data in Reading

Rosemont Reading	Percentage at Level III or IV			Average Scale Score		
	Year 1	Year 2	Year 3	Year 1	Year 2	Year 3
3rd-Grade Reading						
School	64.7	65.2	72.6	143.6	145.7	145.8
Achievement Level III = Scale Score between 141 and 150						
District	72.3	75.1	78.2	146.5	147.1	147.9
Achievement Level IV = Scale Score between 151 and 172						
4th-Grade Reading						
School	57.8	60.6	75	146.1	147.5	150.7
Achievement Level III = Scale Score between 145 and 155						
District	69.4	71.5	73.9	149.7	150.1	150.7
Achievement Level IV = Scale Score between 156 and 174						
5th-Grade Reading						
School	65.7	66.3	68.2	153.6	151.6	153
Achievement Level III = Scale Score between 149 and 158						
District	75.4	82.1	81.4	154.9	156.2	156.1
Achievement Level IV = Scale Score between 159 and 178						
District End-of-5th-Grade Goals						
Goal					Result	
95% of all Grade 5 students will perform on grade level in Reading					68.2	
50% of all Grade 5 students will perform on Level IV in Reading					28.4	

SOURCE: Paul Changas.

Looking first at the percentage of third-grade students who achieved proficiency in reading, it is clear that in Year 1, 64.7 percent of the third-grade students at Rosemont achieved grade-level proficiency. This is compared to 72.3 percent of the average third-grade students in the district who performed at Levels III and IV. You may note that in the following academic years, the percentage of third-grade students who achieved proficiency at Rosemont continued to be lower than the average district percentages. In fact, in every grade level at Rosemont, except for the fourth graders in Year 3, the percentage of students at Level III or IV in reading scored below the district average across all three years.

Let's next look at the trends that these data indicate. You should notice that in third, fourth, and fifth grades at Rosemont, the percentage of students performing at Level III or Level IV increased. However, in fifth grade the percentage of students who achieved proficiency did not increase as much as it did in the other grades. It is important to remember that this comparison of the grade levels across academic years is looking at *different* groups of students each year. That is, the third graders taking the test in Year 1 are different than those third graders who took the test in Year 2.

As a principal, you are likely to be concerned that your third and fifth graders consistently score well below the district average. Fifth grade should be a particular focus. What is going on at this grade level? Has there been significant teacher turnover? Have curricular changes been made? What is the nature of instruction in these classes?

The data on Table 4.6 also allow us to follow a group of students by looking at the data on the diagonal. For example, we can examine a group of third graders in Year 1 and follow this group as fourth graders in Year 2 and as fifth graders in Year 3. This method is called following a *cohort* of students. It is important to note that the cohorts in this table do not remain exactly the same throughout because some students likely leave, and some students come into the school.

For example, 64.7 percent of the third graders in Year 1 were proficient compared with 60.6 percent of these students as fourth graders in Year 2 and 68.2 percent of these students as fifth graders in Year 3. The next cohort of third graders made better progress between their third grade and fourth grade in terms of closing the gap with other students in the district. Specifically, in third grade in Year 2, 65.2 percent of the students were at achievement Level III or IV, and as fourth graders in Year 3, 75 percent of the students achieved at Level III or IV in reading. As you may notice, a larger percentage of these fourth graders at Rosemont performs at grade level than does the average students in the district. Clearly, we may want to know more about what happened at the fourth-grade level to improve the students' proficiency.

The final data to examine on this table are the district end-of-fifth-grade goals. The district has two goals for students at the end of fifth grade in reading: the first is that 95 percent of all fifth-grade students will perform at grade level in reading, and the second is that 50 percent of all fifth-grade students will perform on Level IV, or will exceed expectations, in reading. Notice that it is reported that 68.2 percent of fifth graders have met the first district goal. Can you see where this number came from on Table 4.6? The value of 68.2 percent is the percentage of fifth-grade students in Year 3 at Rosemont who performed at Level III or IV. Clearly, Rosemont has not yet met the first goal set by the district. In addition, Rosemont has not met the second goal set by the district, with only 28.4 percent of the fifth graders performing at Level IV in reading. You may have noted that this value is not found elsewhere in the table; the percentages in the table are a combination of students who have met either Level III or IV.

Disaggregated Data for Elementary Reading Scores

Let's now look at a set of reading data that has been disaggregated by race and lunch code for each grade level. If you recall, this is very important because NCLB requires all students to make adequate yearly progress. It is important to analyze and understand how subgroups of students are achieving on the accountability measures that are part of NCLB. These data are presented in Table 4.7. In fourth grade, in Year 1, 91.7 percent of the white students at Rosemont performed at Level III or IV, whereas only 44.7 percent of the African American students and 41.7 percent of the students characterized by "Other" performed at the proficient level. In Grade 5 you may notice similar academic achievement gaps between the racial groups. The data suggest that there is an achievement gap based on race at Rosemont. The racial gap is not isolated to Year 1. In each year a higher percentage of white students perform at the proficient level than both African American and Other students in every grade.

Let's now look at the disaggregated data by lunch code in the Year 1 school year. In fourth grade only 40.7 percent of the students in the free and reduced-price lunch program perform at the proficient level, as opposed to 89.7 percent of the students who pay for their lunch. You will notice that this pattern continues in Grade 5 as well as in every grade in the other academic years. Clearly, there is also an achievement gap at Rosemont based on participation in the lunch program.

Next we will consider the disaggregated data across academic years. In Grades 4 and 5, the percentage of students who achieve at Level III or IV increases in each racial group.

Table 4.7 Disaggregated Reading Scores

	Year 1	Year 2	Year 3	Year 1	Year 2	Year 3
4th-Grade Reading						
School	57.8	60.6	75	146.1	147.5	150.7
			Achievement Level III = Scale Score between 145 and 155			
District	69.4	71.5	73.9	149.7	150.1	150.7
			Achievement Level IV = Scale Score between 156 and 174			
Race						
African American	44.7	39.6	67.5	142.7	143.1	147.7
White	91.7	100	94.1	155.2	157.1	157.7
Other	41.7	54.5	72.7	141.1	142.8	150.4
Lunch Code						
Free/Reduced	40.7	34.6	60.5	141.3	141.7	146.1
Paid	89.7	92.9	93.3	155.1	154.7	156.4
5th-Grade Reading						
School	65.7	66.3	68.2	153.6	151.6	153
			Achievement Level III = Scale Score between 149 and 158			
District	75.4	82.1	81.4	154.9	156.2	156.1
			Achievement Level IV = Scale Score between 159 and 178			
Race						
African American	43.9	62.5	54.2	147.9	149.5	149.8
White	97.6	85.7	100	162.2	159	160.6
Other	60	44.4	50	150.9	147.3	148.1
Lunch Code						
Free/Reduced	41.1	53.7	45.8	147.5	148.5	147.9
Paid	92.3	87.5	95	160.1	156.9	159.2

SOURCE: Paul Changas.

Remember that the comparison across academic years is looking at different groups of students each year. For example, the percentage of African American fifth graders who perform at the proficient level increases from 43.9 percent in Year 1 to 54.2 percent in Year 3. Remember that the district goal is to have 95 percent of all fifth-grade students performing at grade level in reading. At the end of Year 3, only the white students at Rosemont achieved the district goal. The disaggregated data demonstrate that the educators and administrators at Rosemont need to be concerned about the proficiency levels of African American and Other students.

Let's now look at the trend across the years for the lunch code. For example, in Grade 5 the percentage of students participating in the free and reduced-price lunch program who achieved Level III or IV made a small increase from 41.1 percent in Year 1 to 45.8 percent Year 3. Compared to the larger increases in percentage of free and reduced-price lunch students in fourth grades who achieved proficiency, these data may indicate that Rosemont is not making the necessary changes to improve the achievement levels of lower-income students in Grade 5.

If you recall, the data on this table allow us to follow a group of students, or a cohort, by examining the data on the diagonal. For example, let's follow the group of African American students who are in third grade in Year 1 (not shown in the table). Forty-nine percent of the third grade African American students performed at grade level in Year 1. As fourth graders the percentage decreased to 39.6 percent of the African American students achieving proficiency in Year 2. And as fifth graders the African American students increased the percentage, achieving Level III or IV to 54.2 percent, but still not enough to meet the district goal. It is important to remember that NCLB requires meeting performance targets for each subgroup, so these analyses are central to NCLB accountability goals.

Next we will follow the cohort of free and reduced-price lunch students who were in third grade in Year 1 (not shown in the table). Thirty-three percent of the free and reduced-price lunch students performed at grade level in third grade. This cohort slightly increased in percentage in fourth grade to 34.6 percent, as well as in fifth grade to 45.8 percent. Notice that this cohort did not meet the district goal.

Having conducted a disaggregated review of the school-level data in reading at Rosemont, you have likely noticed patterns of concern such as the academic achievement gaps based on racial groups and income levels. You may have also noticed areas where Rosemont appears to have made efforts to improve student performance such as with the fourth graders in Year 3. This example provides a solid endorsement of the many ways that standardized achievement tests can be used to provide a summative assessment of student and teacher progress within your school.

Limitations of Standardized Tests

Standardized achievement tests have a number of limitations (Koretz, 2002). First is the assumption that a student's score on a test is a "direct and unambiguous measure of student achievement" (Koretz, 2002, p. 754). This is problematic in a number of ways. One problem is the extent to which the test captures and covers the domain it is trying to measure. For example, what should be covered in the domain of eighth-grade mathematics? Typically, the test items used to cover the domain are narrow. Second, because a test cannot completely cover the domain (eighth-grade mathematics), often aspects of the domain that are difficult to assess are not included. "Factual information, for example, and knowledge of simple mathematical procedures are easier to test than problem-solving ability creatively in approaching problems, or deep understandings. These constraints lessen the quality of a test's representation of its domain" (Koretz, 2002, p. 756). A consequence of this limitation is that results from tests that purport to measure the same domain may be markedly different.

A second limitation of standardized tests is that they are not sufficiently aligned to the curriculum standards and instructional emphases in a particular setting or locale. Many standardized tests are created by national companies or organizations, but there is much curricular diversity in the United States. There can be mismatching between what's taught and what's tested (Popham, 2006). Furthermore, it is not clear whose standards are represented in standardized tests.

Standardized testing is a single, one-shot moment in time, usually at the end of the school year. Test scores can be related to out-of-school factors. Value-added assessments systems are one mechanism to try to take these factors into account and level the playing field. As will be explained in next chapter, there are other ways to assess student learning that are embedded within instruction and provide ongoing multiple types of data and information that can help improve instruction and learning.

CONCLUSION

It is important that educational leaders have a solid grasp of the technical aspects of standardized achievement tests, as well as an understanding of the many ways that these data can be harnessed to drive instructional improvement in schools. Schools are accountable under No Child Left Behind for the achievement of all students based on scores on standardized tests. The variety of norm-referenced test scores allows teachers and educational leaders to have a deeper understanding of how their students and their school are performing in relation to important benchmarking groups. Value-added assessment systems are used to measure student growth over time.

The practice of disaggregating data allows for a more fine-grained analysis of how specific subgroups of students are performing. The process of problem-finding and analysis are imperative throughout the process of data-based decision making. This process uses data from multiple sources to determine if student needs are being met and to understand the various factors such as teachers' expertise and school culture that are part of the explanation for low achievement.

In addition to criterion- and norm-referenced achievement tests, there is a host of other measures of student achievement that are important to consider when assessing learning outcomes. Although this chapter has focused on utilizing summative performance data, it is also important to harness the clarifying power of data within a curricular unit. Thus we now turn to the important issue of formative assessment in Chapter 5.

Discussion Questions

1. In comparison to the level of analysis provided in the chapter, to what degree are you currently utilizing disaggregated data to drive instructional improvements in your classroom and school?

2. Provide a brief rationale for why each of the four types of norm-referenced test scores highlighted in Table 4.3 is important. Which one of the four do you most utilize in your current role?

3. Discuss a hunch or perception that you have had about your school that was later confirmed or altered based on a detailed analysis of pertinent data.

4. Discuss your current understanding of limitations on the use of standardized achievement tests.

Using Formative Assessments to Improve Instruction

There are many types of assessments systems that provide teachers with measures of student learning throughout the year rather than waiting for the results of standardized achievement assessments that occur once a year. The logic of these ongoing assessments systems, or what is called *formative assessments systems*, is that they provide teachers with ongoing information regarding their students that can help teachers diagnose specific areas of need and thus teachers can modify instruction. Formative assessments are also used to provide the basis for powerful professional development that is linked to specific learning goals for students. In this chapter you will learn about formative assessments and their role in the school-improvement process.

VIGNETTE REVISITED

As the new principal at Rosemont School, you know the importance of your students' performance on standardized achievement tests. Your staff has acquired a solid knowledge and understanding of how the school is being held accountable for adequate yearly progress. Yet your staff and leadership team understand that standardized achievement testing occurs only once a year and does not provide adequate diagnostic information about whether students are mastering standards and learning objectives as the school year progresses. In addition, teachers are not receiving feedback regarding common areas of difficulty across grade levels and subject matters. Teachers have also begun to note

---

the limitations of standardized tests and have expressed interest in other types of assessments that measure learning that cannot be captured by year-end tests. You begin to explore the inclusion of formative assessments and other nonstandardized measures of learning into your school-improvement processes.

NONSTANDARDIZED MEASURES OF ACHIEVEMENT

As discussed previously, schools are held accountable for student learning. Although end-of-year achievement tests are one measure of achievement, student learning is measured most often by teacher-made tests. These nonstandardized measures of achievement are often used as mechanisms for summative evaluation, that is, to make a final judgment about mastery of course objectives and content material, such as assigning a final grade. This is often referred to as *mastery measurement*.

However, these nonstandardized teacher-made assessments are often used for formative feedback as well. Other formative assessments include districtwide testing programs and portfolios. Formative evaluations, assessments, or measurements are used to provide ongoing feedback during the learning process. Formative assessments can provide feedback to both teachers and students about students' progress and understanding of content. Formative assessments provide information about areas that need additional practice or reteaching. Formative assessments are an essential part of the teaching and learning process that provides detailed feedback about what material is and what material is not mastered. In this sense formative assessments are very helpful in diagnosing gaps and helping teachers focus and differentiate instruction.

Beyond teacher-made assessments, additional types of formative assessments that help gauge student learning outcomes include district- and school-developed tests. Recently districts have begun adopting commercially available formative assessment systems as well. These assessments are linked to state standards.

Even though standardized achievement tests play an important role in data-based decision making, ongoing classroom assessments must be used for continuous monitoring and feedback to drive instructional change. Standardized achievement tests and formative classroom assessments should be used hand-in-hand to drive instruction, and both types of assessments are integral to the data-based decision-making process. Often the distinction is made that summative assessments such as standardized tests entail assessment *OF* learning, while formative assessments are assessments *FOR* learning.

Previously we provided examples of how standardized achievement tests are used to clarify the knowledge domains and skills students have not mastered. Formative assessments can also be used to diagnose mastery of specific curricular aims and skills. The information gleaned from formative assessments can help teachers plan instruction and reteaching of areas not mastered. Formative tests can then be used to reassess the extent to which specific curricular aims have been mastered. Formative assessments should be an integral part of the teaching and learning process to enhance learning. In fact, research has shown that formative assessment is a powerful mechanism for raising student performance (Black & Wiliam, 1998a, 1998b).

Formative assessments are compiled and written by the teacher or a local group of teachers and can also be developed at the district level or by outside vendors such as a commercial company. As stated previously formative assessments are used to assess students during the school year to plan instructional interventions. As such, formative assessments must be administered multiple times during the school year, if not multiple times within a particular curricular unit.

The information from formative assessments can also be used to determine areas and topics for faculty professional development for the school. Thus the advantage of developing a collaborative mechanism in the school to administer similar formative assessments is to use the information to focus professional development and to develop teams of teachers to plan instruction together to target instruction for standards that emerge as problematic or causing difficulty both within grades and across grade levels.

Often district-level formative assessments have computerized reporting mechanisms that help teachers identify groups of students who struggle with the same standards, to identify students who are in the greatest need of remedial help, and to facilitate collaboration. Some commercial companies are developing the notion of formative assessments as *predictive assessments*. The software uses the formative assessment results to try to predict how close students are to meeting state standards on the standardized achievement tests. Formative assessments can also engage students in charting their own learning.

Research suggests that schools that use student assessment results to guide instruction make progress in improving student achievement (Snipes, Doolittle, & Herlihy, 2002). However, merely implementing formative assessments is not sufficient. Formative assessments are best used when they promote a dialogue among teachers and a focus on professional development. "Identifying patterns in student assessment results is only a first step. A second is brainstorming about possible explanations. A third is developing and implementing a strategy for identifying the most compelling explanation. Often this requires collection and examination of other data, such as student writing samples and student attendance patterns" (Sharkey & Murnane, 2006, p. 576). In other words, the use of formative assessments, like other data, requires problem-finding techniques.

In fact, research suggests a strong association between using data and a professional culture in schools. Using data is an empowering process (Chrispeels, Brown, & Castillo, 2000); it helps open up the dialogue among educators in the school to become more collaborative (Feldman & Tung, 2001) and more collaborative across departments (Nichols & Singer, 2000).

In sum, the use of ongoing formative assessments can be used to chart progress and continually diagnose teaching and learning. Formative assessments can be used to:

- Monitor and evaluate student progress
- Identify specific learning needs by subject matter, grade levels, groups of students, and groups of teachers
- Disaggregate data for planning and comparing to NCLB
- Plan professional development and identify teachers who can support and help other teachers
- Change and monitor instructional practices
- Plan and implement differentiated instruction to meet individual students' needs and learning goals
- Provide feedback to students about their learning and engage them in setting learning goals (Boston, 2002; Guskey, 2003)

It is helpful for the leadership in a school to have a clear, compelling vision about the use of formative assessments. Figure 5.1 presents an example of a vision that makes very clear why and how formative assessments are used in the school.

Figure 5.1 Memphis City Public Schools' Vision Statement

Formative Assessment System Vision

- To validate and ensure that the goals of instruction are being achieved and to improve instruction when necessary

- To monitor our students' learning and our own teaching practices

- To identify students' individual growth, classroom instructional outcomes, school collaborative planning needs, and district professional development focus

SOURCE: Memphis City School District. http://www.mcsk12.net/admin/tlapages /literacy_sec/renlearning/index.asp

- To promote consistency and alignment of the district curricula as well as the state blueprint

Formative Tests

Figure 5.2 provides an example of the type of information that can be gleaned from commercially derived formative tests. The example provided is linked to the Tennessee State Standards.

Figure 5.2 Example of Formative Data From a Commercial Provider

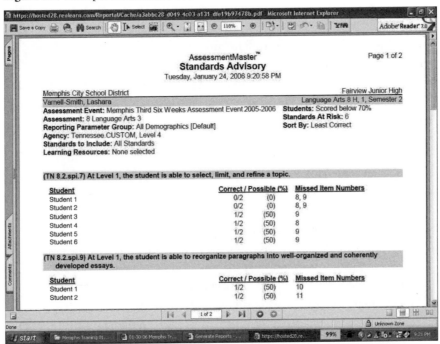

SOURCE: Memphis City School District. http://www.mcsk12.net/admin/tlapages /literacy_sec/renlearning/documents/AssessmentMaster_Teacher_Manual.pdf

The information is organized by the specific standards being assessed such as the following: "The student is able to select, limit, and refine a topic" or "The student is able to reorganize paragraphs into well-organized and coherently developed essays." From this assessment we learn that six students have not mastered the first standard, two students missed the two items that assess this standard, and four students missed one of the two items. It is important to note that only two items assessed this standard; therefore, the teacher should use other information to judge the extent to which these students have difficulty with this standard. Other information should include student work, authentic examples of actual writing, teacher-made tests and assessments, and so on.

Curriculum-Based Measurement

Curriculum-based measurement (CBM) is one type of formative assessment used for continual progress monitoring that has been the subject of widespread scientifically based research. CBM is a set of standardized and validated short-duration tests that are used by teachers for identifying students in need of additional and different forms of instruction (Fuchs & Fuchs, n.d.). CBM has been implemented in reading, spelling, and mathematics, primarily with students with learning disabilities, but is now being implemented more and more with general education students. The research on CBM indicates that when teachers implement this type of formative assessments, students learn more, teachers are better able to make instructional decisions, and students are more aware of their own learning performance (Fuchs, Deno, & Mirkin, 1984).

As summarized by noted researchers Lynn and Doug Fuchs, curriculum-based measurement is different from typical classroom assessments, termed *mastery assessments*:

> With mastery measurements, teachers test for mastery of a single skill and, after mastery is demonstrated, they assess mastery of the next skill in a sequence. So, at different times of the school year, different skills are assessed. Because the nature and difficulty of the tests keep changing with successive mastery, test scores from different times of the year cannot be compared. This makes it impossible to quantify or describe rates of progress. Furthermore, mastery measures have unknown reliability and validity, and it fails to provide information about whether students are maintaining the previously mastered skills. (n.d., p. 1)

In contrast to mastery measurement, curriculum-based measurement assesses skills covered throughout the curriculum at various points throughout each year. Using different items, these formative assessments continually assess the skills that need to be mastered for the year so that "scores earned at different items during the school year can be compared to determine whether a student's competence is increasing." "CBM is *dynamic* in that the measures are designed to be sensitive to the short-term effects (i.e., 4–6 weeks) of instructional interventions; they are designed to assess *change*" (Shinn, 2002, p. 675).

As the example in Figure 5.3 suggests, CBM can be used with a whole class to monitor instructional progress. It can be used to screen and to identify students who may need extra instruction or a different type of instruction. For students not progressing from the typical instructional program, alternative teaching and instructional strategies can be implemented. The results of CBM assessment in Figure 5.3 suggest that some students (a small group) need additional instruction on subtraction. Additionally, many students in the class would benefit from additional instruction on multiplying two digits.

Figure 5.3 Classroom Summary of Curriculum-Based Measurement in Mathematics

Class Summary

Teacher: Mrs. Smith
Report through 3/17

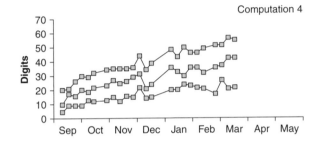

Students to Watch

Jonathan Nichols
Amanda Ramirez
Anthony Jones
Erica Jernigan
Wayne Campbell

Most Improved

Chris Carter
Michael Elliott
Jonathan Nichols
Michael Sanders
Matthew Hayes

Areas of Improvement: Computation

M1 Multiplying basic facts
M2 Multiplying by 1 digit
M3 Multiplying by 2 digits
D1 Dividing basic facts

Whole Class Instruction: Computation

M3 Multiplying by 2 digits
58% of your students are either COLD or COOL on this skill.

Small Group Instruction: Computation

S1 Subtracting
Cindy Lincoln
Ben Ross
Kaitlin Laird
Michael Elliott
Michael Sanders

SOURCE: Fuchs, L. S., Fuchs, D., & Courey, S. J. (2005). Curriculum-based measurement of mathematics competence: From computation to concepts and applications to real-life problem solving. *Assessment for Effective Instruction, 30*(2), 33–46.

Teacher Classroom Assessments

Classroom assessments such as quizzes, tests, assignments, and other student work products provide important information that can guide improvements in instruction and student learning (Guskey, 2003a). Guskey suggests three specific issues that need to be addressed for classroom assessments to be useful sources of data. First, the content of the assessments should be aligned with both the instructional emphases in the classroom and state and district standards. Second, the assessments should provide useful information to teachers that can help them identify what they taught well and what needs to be retaught Third, the assessments "must be followed by high quality, corrective instruction designed to remedy whatever learning errors the assessment identified" (Guskey, p. 7). Thus, as is the case with all formative assessments, simply grading student work does not help improve instruction; teachers must act on the data.

Portfolios

Portfolios are another type of assessment of student learning using student work. A *portfolio* is a collection of a student's work demonstrating mastering and accomplishments. Portfolios usually include students' self-reflection and teachers' evaluations of their work. Portfolios are often termed *authentic* or *performance based* because these assessments are based on actual demonstration of student work rather than a test. Authentic assessments are "performance assessment in which the student's tasks resembles real-life tasks" (Popham, 2006, p. 233). Portfolios are not limited to a one-time showing of knowledge, like a test, but include an accumulation of student work and projects over time. According to the Northwest Evaluation Association, a portfolio is "a purposeful collection of student work that exhibits the student's effort, progress and achievements. The collection must include student participation in selecting the contents, the criteria for selection, the criteria for judging merit, and evidence of student self-reflection" (Paulson, Paulson, & Meyer, 1991). Portfolios and other student work also provide a mechanism for teachers and students to build a common understanding around educational outcomes. Questions to address include the following: What should be included in a portfolio? What counts as evidence of student learning and achievement? What rubric will be used to score and assess the portfolio?

Portfolios, therefore, are not a random collection of work but are comprised of products associated with specific instructional goals across subject matters. Portfolios help document a student's learning and progress. Portfolios can include materials beyond written work such as projects, videos, audiotapes, and so forth. Building the portfolio is an integral part of the learning and assessment process because it involves collaboration between the teachers and the students.

Key to effectively implementing portfolio assessments is portfolio evaluation and the feedback mechanism. Portfolios as a whole, as well as specific pieces of student work in the portfolio, are typically evaluated using performance rubrics. A *rubric* is "a scoring guide used to evaluate the quality of students' constructed responses. A rubric has three essential components: evaluation criteria, quality definitions, and a scoring strategy" (Popham, 2006, p. 238). A performance rubric usually includes evaluation criteria through a matrix with levels of performance from "distinguished" to "not acceptable." Specific details about what level of and type of work meets the performance criteria are part of each rubric. This makes the nature of the assessment very clear and visible to everyone. Rubrics also serve as a guidepost for students so they can develop their assignments and self-assess their work. An example of a performance rubric for assessing math performance is provided in Figure 5.4.

Shared active feedback is an important aspect of portfolio assessments. Students can have individual and group feedback conferences where progress is discussed and goals are set for future meetings. In this way portfolio assessments play a formative feedback role. The portfolios can also be used as summative assessments as a final accumulation of products of the student's work at the end of the semester or school year. As such, portfolios provide another indicator of whether the school is meeting high standards of learning and achievement for all students.

Developing Teacher Capacity to Use Formative Assessments

As a school leader, you help to develop the conditions that can facilitate the effective use of formative data for instructional improvement. Three aspects necessary for developing data use amongst teachers are professional development, supportive data climate, and collaboration (Wyman, 2005).

Professional development. Leaders cannot assume that teachers know how to use formative data. Furthermore, leaders cannot assume that teachers know how to link summative and formative data to make instructional decisions. Teachers typically are not prepared to "view their craft and their students' learning through the information lens" (Wyman, 2005, p. 301). It is important that professional development for data use be embedded in the ongoing, regular work of teachers at the local school site. While districtwide or larger-scale professional development opportunities

Figure 5.4 Scoring Rubric for Mathematics Performance Assessment

4   *Mathematical knowledge:* Demonstrates an understanding of the problem's mathematical concepts; uses algorithms correctly with appropriate terminology and notations. Problem completed without errors.
Strategic knowledge: Identifies and shows the relationship between important elements; all problem-solving steps presented in sequential order with supporting evidence of solution.
Communication: Clear, complete explanation of the problem-solving process with strong solution support. Diagrams may be included to support explanations.

3   *Mathematical knowledge:* Demonstrates an understanding of most of the problem's mathematical concepts; uses algorithms correctly with most of the appropriate terminology and notations. Completed problem may have minor errors.
Strategic knowledge: Identifies and shows the relationship between most important elements; most problem-solving steps presented in sequential order with most supporting evidence of solution.
Communication: Reasonably completes explanation of the problem-solving process with some gaps in solution support. Diagrams included support most of the explanations.

2   *Mathematical knowledge:* Demonstrates an understanding of some of the problem's mathematical concepts; contains algorithm errors; terminology and notations are incomplete. Problem may have major computation errors.
Strategic knowledge: Identifies some of the relationship between important elements; problem-solving steps are incomplete without sequential order or supporting evidence.
Communication: Reasonable attempt made to solve the problem. The explanation of problem-solving process has gaps and is unclear. Diagrams included are unclear or lack support.

1   *Mathematical knowledge:* Demonstrates little understanding of the problem's mathematical concepts; contains algorithm errors; terminology and notations are incorrect. Problem has major computation errors.
Strategic knowledge: Important elements are not identified; problem-solving steps are incomplete, inappropriate, and/or without sequential order.
Communication: Some attempt made to solve the problem. The explanation of problem-solving process is unclear or inappropriate. Diagrams included are unclear and may misinterpret the problem.

0   *Mathematical knowledge:* Demonstrates no understanding of the problem's mathematical concepts.
Strategic knowledge: Lacking or insignificant problem-solving strategies. Little or no evidence of attempt to solve problem.
Communication: Explanation unrelated to problem.

SOURCE: Sandra Burvikovs, Lake Zurich Public Schools, Illinois.

may be informative, successful implementation of ongoing data use for instructional improvement requires teacher-to-teacher interactions and teachers talking about the data, implications of the data, and specific suggestion on how to alter instruction to meet individual students' learning needs. Developing teachers who can provide local support to other teachers is an important step for developing teacher leader capacity around using data. Wyman suggests the importance of classroom coaches, data facilitators, and data mentors. Certainly there may be technological needs in helping teachers access formative assessments and other data reports, but much of the emphases of these supports can be on interpretation and use of data for instructional decision making. In fact, recent research suggests that teachers are not "data-phobic but rather that they don't have recent experience in working with data to improve specific classroom practices" (Ingram, Louis, & Schroeder, 2004, p. 1280), reinforcing the need for professional development.

Supportive data climates. Leaders must both model the use of data and encourage and support teachers in their use of data for instructional improvement. In this regard, a climate of trust is paramount. As noted by Ingram and colleagues (2004), teachers will be reluctant to use data if "there are judgmental consequences and punitive retributions" (p. 1276). The cultures of many schools do not lend themselves to the mode of problem finding that is central to supporting teachers' use of data. Ingram and colleagues highlight four cultural barriers to teachers' use of data than can be overcome through strong leadership that supports a culture of data. One barrier is that many teachers have their own notions of the effectiveness of their teaching that is not consistent with that provided by outside sources of information and data. A second barrier is that teachers make their decisions based on intuition and anecdotal information. A third barrier is that there may be disagreement in the school about what data are meaningful and important for improving instruction and student learning. And the fourth barrier is that some teachers separate their own teaching from the learning of their students, thus overlooking useful and important data.

Leaders aware of these potential barriers can develop relationships with teachers and teacher leaders to help overcome them. For example, when discussing specific students, asking teachers to show the data will help develop a culture that goes beyond anecdotes and intuition. Leaders should create opportunities and time for teachers to share how they have used data and how it has changed their instructional practices and how students have learned. These opportunities can be developed through scheduling grade-level and subject-matter teams, integrated teams for vertical alignment, and teams focusing on specific problems or pathways such as family involvement or safety. The important issue is to provide teachers with the time and space to support one another in their use of data.

Collaboration. Closely related to the idea of a school culture that supports data is the notion that collaboration is important for teachers to adopt the use of data for instructional improvement. The educational change research has noted that collaboration is a key ingredient for implementing and sustaining changes in teachers' practices. Working with data is no different. Teachers who can exchange ideas and practices and share frustrations and difficulties are much more likely to both adopt the practice as well as sustain its use. Collaboration can take many formats. The most obvious format is meetings and discussions about specific data, what they mean, and how they can be used to improve instruction. Other forms of collaboration include visiting teachers' classrooms to see how teachers have differentiated instruction based on results of formative assessments. Teachers can collaborate on developing formative assessment measures as well, such as designing student assignments to illicit information surrounding students' mastery and learning of specific standards, or developing rubrics for critiquing student writing.

Collaboration around data is an effective strategy to distribute leadership among teachers and administrators (Copeland, 2003). Copeland described schools that are advanced in their problem-finding inquiry and data-use strategies as nested layers of collaboration with teams

> maturing into an accepted, iterative process of data collection, analysis, reflection and change. . . . Discourse about students' standards-based achievement and expectations about evidence are commonplace rather than the exception. Leadership for change comes from within the school growing out of the inquiry process. Teachers' new knowledge about how students do across groups and across grades appears to enable them to see ways in which they need to improve, and the kinds of resources they need to begin making these improvements. (p. 387)

CONCLUSION

Formative assessments are powerful data-based decision-making tools if they are used to inform the instructional practices for teachers and the learning experiences for students. This chapter has provided several suggestions regarding the utilization of school and classroom data as formative assessments of student learning. The chapter highlighted the importance of a schoolwide or systemwide vision for formative assessment as well as a clear understanding of various purposes that can be served by the using formative forms of data. Additionally, the chapter described benefits associated with particular types of formative assessments such as curriculum-based measurement. School leaders can help teachers understand the purposes and uses of formative assessments. No less important, however, is for leaders to help create and support the conditions for the use of teacher classroom assessments for formative purposes. Professional development, a supportive data climate, and opportunities for collaboration are key ingredients to support the use of formative assessments.

Discussion Questions

1. Comment on the degree to which you, or the teachers in your school, currently use formative student assessment results to guide instruction.

2. On page 80, a summary of seven uses of formative assessment is listed. Rate your current school on each of these seven dimensions along a scale from "minimal" to "substantial."

3. Craft a formative assessment system vision statement, similar to the one shown in Figure 5.1, appropriate for your school or district.

4. When describing teacher classroom assessments, three specific issues were discussed that have implications for making classroom assessments useful. Rate the current effectiveness of your school in each of these three areas and set a goal for enhancing the performance in one of these domains.

5. List two benefits and two challenges associated with utilizing portfolio assessments.

6. The chapter discusses three aspects that can encourage data use among teachers: professional development, supportive data climate, and collaboration. Choose one of these three areas and describe several concrete ways a school leader can implement this aspect to facilitate data use among teachers in your school.

Multiple Measures for Pathways to School Improvement

What data are necessary for school-improvement planning? Drawing upon the key indicators of successful schools, this chapter discusses the various types and sources of data that address the key factors that help leaders propel teaching and learning. Education leaders must rely heavily on ongoing analyses of these school-improvement indicators for both school-improvement planning and data-based decision making. At the end of this chapter, you should be able to describe the numerous types of data that education leaders can employ to monitor school progress using the effective school indicators.

VIGNETTE REVISITED

The leadership team at Rosemont School now has a deeper understanding of how standardized and teacher-made test data can be used to measure student achievement. Yet, as the principal of Rosemont, you understand that these types of data provide only a partial picture of student, faculty, and school success. To anchor the collection of additional data, the leadership team decides to focus on school-improvement indicators. The team, however, is overwhelmed by the myriad of data sources that could potentially be used to assess their faculty, student, and school progress.

In addition to measuring student outcomes, it is important to use data to measure school processes that are associated with student learning and achievement. If a school community does not know how they measure up on key pathways associated with student achievement, they will not know which pathways or processes need to be changed and enhanced. In other words, data are collected on the key pathways to student learning to answer the *why* questions: Why are fifth-grade students not achieving as much as fourth-grade students are? Why is writing lagging behind all other indicators in your school? To answer these why questions, you would want to know if, for example, the fifth-grade teachers are less likely to have a common planning time than other teachers are. Is the writing curriculum less aligned with the standards than other subjects are? Is there less parental involvement in fifth grade than there is in fourth grade? This chapter describes the manner in which you can collect the types of data necessary to answer the why questions often raised by a thorough analysis of various types of student achievement data.

In Chapter 2 we discussed in detail the common indicators, or pathways, to successful schools. We mentioned that these pathways identify important types of data that are central to data-based decision making for school improvement. The paths are many, but the key areas of focus are attention to the school's mission and goals; rigorous content standards for all students; curricular and instructional coherence and alignment to standards; expert teachers supported by coherent, consistent professional development; partnerships with parents, families, and community; the professional community of teachers; the climate of the school; and resources aligned to goals. Within this discussion we cited the importance of benchmarking as a starting point in data-based decision making. In this chapter we will review each of the key pathways to school improvement and discuss various types and sources of data that can be used to benchmark and gauge how well your school is implementing the key pathways to successful schools. Armed with data about student outcomes and key pathways to those outcomes, you and your school community will be ready to set forth a plan for school improvement and be in a position to continuously monitor and evaluate progress toward your school's key goals.

SHARED MISSION AND GOALS

As described in detail in Chapter 3, the mission and goals of a school play a pivotal role in guiding the curricular and programmatic activities of the school. What follows is a condensed version, which may serve as a nice review, of ways that you may collect and analyze data regarding the key purposes driving an educational organization. Although a school mission is generally a broad and somewhat established set of guiding principles, the goals of the organization can undergo yearly alterations based on school-level or broader policy initiatives. There is considerable evidence that a key function of effective school leadership concerns shaping the purpose of the school or articulating the school's mission (Bamburg & Andrews, 1990; Hallinger & Heck, 2002; Murphy, Elliott, Goldring, & Porter, 2007). Traditionally, this aspect of leadership focused primarily on the principal's role in ensuring that the school has clear, measurable goals for student learning and academic progress. Setting clear goals for student achievement is central to effective leadership because it guides daily practices and decisions of all stakeholders. Because the school mission and goals play such a pivotal role for the organization, it is important that school leaders understand the degree to which these aspirations are being attained. A first step in this process is to consider the measurable components of the school mission and then determine the types and sources of data that speak to each particular component. This process can be facilitated by using a matrix such as the one provided in Table 6.1.

Table 6.1 Data Sources Pertinent to Mission Statement

What the Mission Statement Says	Data We Already Have to Measure the Mission Statement	Data We Need to Collect to Measure the Mission Statement

SOURCE: Adapted from Holcomb, E. (2002). *Getting Excited About Data*. Corwin Press, Thousand Oaks, CA.

For example, consider the mission statement of Rosemont School, as noted in Chapter 3:

> The mission of Rosemont School is to provide a safe and secure environment and provide opportunities for all students to perform at or above grade level in reading, writing, and mathematics while demonstrating responsibility and self-control.

A first step in using this matrix to analyze the degree to which your mission statement is being fulfilled may be to assemble a team. Once you have assembled a team, the team's first task would be to list the various components of the mission statement in the left column of the matrix. Next, the team would need to prioritize and analyze the existing data you have for your school pertinent to each component of the mission statement. The purpose here is to develop a sense of the overall picture of the school as a starting point, relying on data you already have. These data will be used to benchmark the school's mission to determine the components of the mission being attained and those with the greatest need. These analyses will pinpoint areas for further analysis and exploration and focusing change efforts.

Where components of the mission are not being assessed by existing data, the leadership team may decide to construct data-gathering instruments to pinpoint these domains. For example, if there are no existing data regarding the degree to which students are demonstrating responsibility, you can craft an instrument that directly addresses this issue.

RIGOROUS CONTENT STANDARDS FOR ALL STUDENTS

In today's policy environment, it is imperative that all students are presented with rigorous content and held to high standards of achievement. Current research contends that we not only assess the mere presence of standards for student learning but also specifically emphasize the quality of the school goals, namely, the extent to which there are high standards and rigorous learning goals (Goldring, Porter, Murphy, Elliott, & Cravens, 2007). The research literature has supported the notion that high expectations for all, including clear and public standards, are keys to closing the achievement gap between advantaged and less advantaged students and for raising the overall academic achievements of all students. Early research on effective schools in lower socioeconomic communities found that these schools held high expectations for their students (Brookover & Lezotte, 1979; Purkey & Smith, 1983). More recently Betts and Grogger (2003) found that, on average, higher grading standards are associated with higher twelfth-grade test scores. High standards for student performance focus on outputs rather than processes or inputs (Porter, 1994). In our framework high standards means "they are intended to be absolute rather than normative. Second, they are expected to be set at high, 'world-class' levels. Finally they are expected to apply to all, or essentially all, students rather than a selected subset such as college bound students seeking advanced placement" (Linn, 2000, p. 10).

As such, it is essential that today's educational leaders collect and analyze data that can provide information about the degree to which students—all students—are interacting with quality instructional resources and attaining benchmarks of adequate yearly progress. One place to begin this analysis is to have a solid understanding of your state's framework for academic standards. In addition to state standards, many districts have additional expectations for student and school success. Moreover, as a school community, you will have a targeted, or nuanced, set of standards that guide instructional decisions. To assess the degree to which your school is meeting these multiple layers of expectations, you will need to collect multiple types of data.

The notion of opportunities to learn is important when collecting data regarding the extent to which students are learning a rigorous curriculum of high standards. Key questions include, do all students have access to a rigorous curriculum, or are some students grouped into lower-level classes that are not consistent with the standards? Leaders use data to evaluate the extent to which all students complete a rigorous curricular program and monitor the curriculum through frequent visits to classes. Clear targets of student learning are set for all students.

You can also do a comparison of high- and low-performing students or privileged and low-income students. Do the higher performing students have greater access to school and classroom high standards? Do low-income or minority students have fewer opportunities to benefit from rigorous standards?

Each day educators are determining more ways to harness the capacity to enrich teaching and learning. The primary vehicle by which rigorous content standards can be achieved is through interaction with quality teaching around quality content. Toward this end, and with the assistance of both formal and informal leaders and teachers, you can routinely assess the curricular and pedagogical exposure that all subsets of students in a school experience. Through a combination of observation, document analysis, and survey data, you can determine disparities in student opportunities to learn, which in the contemporary educational policy arena are no longer tolerable.

CURRICULAR AND INSTRUCTIONAL COHERENCE AND ALIGNMENT

It only makes sense that the more efficient an organization is, the greater the payoff will be from the organizational efforts. In the case of schools, coherence between educational experiences and academic expectations is a primary mechanism to enhance efficiency. Although it is important to articulate a worthy mission, establish challenging goals, and set rigorous standards, these are essentially a proposed destination. Without ensuring that the curriculum and instruction are harnessed and engaged in a way that can get you there, the goals and standards will serve only as a reminder of what might have been. As such, it is imperative to ensure that there is a high degree of coherence between the mechanism for student growth, curriculum, and instruction, and the destination articulated in the standards and school goals.

Figure 6.1 illustrates various layers of alignment among standards, assessments, and instruction. Achievement can be more or less aligned to instruction, instruction to district standards and assessments, and district standards and assessments to state standards and assessments. These are all examples of vertical alignment. Horizontal alignment is a measure of the consistency of standards and assessments within a district or state, that is, the degree to which these policy instruments deliver a coherent set of expectations to teachers (Porter, 2002). Alignment is the central idea in systemic, standards-based reform (Smith & O'Day, 1991). Within this framework an instructional system is to be driven by content standards, which are translated into curricular units and assessments. From here curricular materials, instructional lessons, and professional development would ideally be tightly aligned to the content standards. The hypothesis is that a coherent message of desired content will influence teachers' decisions about what to teach, and teachers' decisions, in turn, will translate into instructional practice and ultimately into student learning of the desired content (Porter, 2002).

Figure 6.1 Vertical and Horizontal Alignment

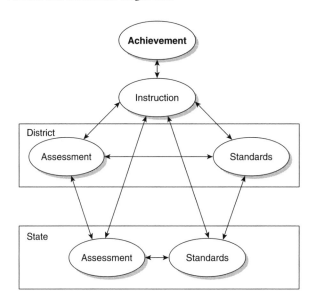

SOURCE: Porter, 2002. Measuring the Content of Instruction: Uses in Research and Practice. *Educational Researcher, 31*(7), pp. 3–14.

One way to ensure a high level of alignment between curriculum and standards is to fill out a content matrix. An example is provided in Table 6.2. Here, for example, you might place the state standards for fifth-grade math students along the top column headers, and along the vertical axis you could place curricular units. Next, you would fill out the degree to which each of the standards was covered within each curricular unit. This would provide a broad-brush picture of the degree of alignment of your math curriculum to the state standards.

Table 6.2 Alignment Matrix

Curricular Topics	Fifth-Grade State Math Standard Components				
	Memorize Facts/ Definitions/ Formulas	Perform Procedures	Demonstrate Understanding	Conjecture/ Generalize	Solve Non-Routine Problems
Place value					
Whole numbers					
Operations					
Fractions					
Decimals					
Percents					
Ratio and proportion					
Patterns					
Real numbers					

SOURCE: Porter, 2002. Measuring the Content of Instruction: Uses in Research and Practice. *Educational Researcher, 31*(7), pp. 3–14.

To supplement this picture, you would want to survey your fifth-grade math teachers regarding the degree to which each of the content standards was covered within a particular unit. Such a survey is provided in Figure 6.2. (For additional information about Surveys of the Enacted Curriculum, see http://seconline.wceruw.org.) These survey data could then be converted into a graphic depiction of the degree of alignment between your fifth-grade mathematics curriculum and the stated standards. Figure 6.3 provides an example of how these data can be graphically displayed. From such a picture of school-level alignment between instruction and standards, an educational leader can make significant progress in assisting grade-level teams fill in any gaps or thin out areas of overcoverage. Additionally, if the root cause for apparent misalignment can be traced to weaknesses in teacher capacity, these data can help an educational leader provide targeted professional development for teachers.

A very important aspect of data-based decision making regarding alignment and coherence is the alignment and coherence across grade levels—called *vertical alignment*. An alignment matrix for each grade is needed to address the question, how are content standards related across grades? Vertical alignment from one grade to the next can be achieved through extending knowledge and skills to a wider range of content, deepening understanding of the same content, including higher cognitive demand, and adding new or different content (U.S. Department of Education, 2006).

Data should address such questions as the following: What new content is required from one grade to the next? How is depth of knowledge and cognitive demand addressed? What knowledge content is a prerequisite for next year's standards?

Figure 6.2 Teacher Survey of Curricular Alignment With State Standards

Time on Topic		Elementary School Mathematics Topics	Expectations for Students in Mathematics				
<none>		Number Sense / Properties /Relationships	Memorize Facts/ Definitions/ Formulas	Perform Procedures	Demonstrate Understanding of Mathematical Ideas	Conjecture, Generalize, Prove	Solve Non-Routine Problems/Make Connections
⓪①②③	101	Place value	⓪①②③	⓪①②③	⓪①②③	⓪①②③	⓪①②③
⓪①②③	102	Patterns	⓪①②③	⓪①②③	⓪①②③	⓪①②③	⓪①②③
⓪①②③	103	Decimals	⓪①②③	⓪①②③	⓪①②③	⓪①②③	⓪①②③
⓪①②③	104	Percent	⓪①②③	⓪①②③	⓪①②③	⓪①②③	⓪①②③
⓪①②③	105	Real numbers	⓪①②③	⓪①②③	⓪①②③	⓪①②③	⓪①②③
⓪①②③	106	Exponents, scientific notation	⓪①②③	⓪①②③	⓪①②③	⓪①②③	⓪①②③
⓪①②③	107	Factors, multiples, divisibility	⓪①②③	⓪①②③	⓪①②③	⓪①②③	⓪①②③
⓪①②③	108	Odds, evens, primes, composites	⓪①②③	⓪①②③	⓪①②③	⓪①②③	⓪①②③
⓪①②③	109	Estimation	⓪①②③	⓪①②③	⓪①②③	⓪①②③	⓪①②③
⓪①②③	110	Order of operations	⓪①②③	⓪①②③	⓪①②③	⓪①②③	⓪①②③
⓪①②③	111	Relationships between operations	⓪①②③	⓪①②③	⓪①②③	⓪①②③	⓪①②③

SOURCE: Porter, 2002. Measuring the Content of Instruction: Uses in Research and Practice. *Educational Researcher, 31*(7), pp. 3–14.

Figure 6.3 Example of Graphic Depiction of Alignment Data

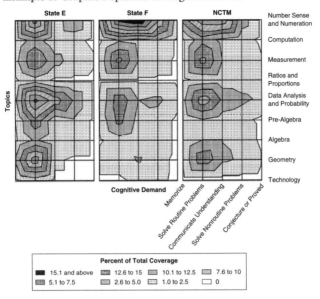

SOURCE: Porter, 2002. Measuring the Content of Instruction: Uses in Research and Practice. *Educational Researcher, 31*(7), pp. 3–14.

EXPERT TEACHERS SUPPORTED BY COHERENT, CONSISTENT PROFESSIONAL DEVELOPMENT

To support school missions that incorporate challenging standards that are aligned to curriculum and instruction, effective schools have teachers dedicated to developing their expertise in curricular content and pedagogy, and create an environment that emphasizes professional learning and development for the entire organization (Darling-Hammond, 2000). Professional development and learning is an ongoing process throughout the school. Professional development provides high quality and relevant content to teachers to help them improve the teaching and learning in their classrooms and creates a culture of expectations and supports for ongoing development and improvement. This statement highlights the key role that professional development plays in the enhancement of teacher quality and the advancement of learning. There is growing recognition that investments aimed at increasing teacher quality are among the most productive means for increasing student learning (Darling-Hammond, 2000; National Commission on Teaching and America's Future, 1996).

Empirical studies have been conducted on the effectiveness of professional development opportunities for teachers. These studies provide insight about both the content and the manner of instruction, or processes, that make professional development experiences beneficial to teachers. For example, Porter, Garet, Desimone, Birman, and Yoon (2003)

contended that there is an emerging consensus in the research literature on the characteristics of effective professional development. Based
on analysis of the research literature and their own empirical work on
professional development, Porter and his colleagues have found consistent support for the following five characteristics of effective professional
development experiences:

1. The content focus of the activity, such as the degree to which the
   activity is focused on enhancing teachers' content knowledge and
   how students learn the content

2. The duration of the activity, including the total number of hours
   that participants spend in the activity, as well as the span of time
   over which the activity takes place

3. The degree to which the activity includes the collective participation of teachers from the same school, department, or grade level

4. The extent to which the activity offers opportunities for active
   learning by the participants

5. The coherence of the activity, both in terms of promoting consistency between teachers' professional development and other
   activities and the degree to which it is aligned with the appropriate standards and assessments

Perhaps most important, professional development must be driven
by analyses of student performance. Analyses of student performance in
the classroom, not just end-of-year standardized tests and the goals and
standards for student learning, are the basis for professional development
(Hawley & Valli, 2007). "Such analyses will define what educators need,
rather than want, to learn, make professional development student-
centered, and increase public confidence in the use of resources for professional development" (p. 120).

Teachers are involved in collaborative problem-finding teams to help
determine how professional development can best address issues uncovered in the data regarding student performance. By involving teachers
in the both the identification of the content of professional development
and the design of the learning opportunities, teachers' commitment and
motivation are enhanced.

One criticism levied against many studies of effective professional
development is the reliance on teacher self-reports as the measure of
change or growth. The lack of evidence from classroom observations that
could verify the self-reported changes in practices actually occurred, or
information that would link these changes to measures of student learning,

is one limitation of this line of inquiry (Guskey, 2003b). As such, an educational leader would be well advised to collect both self-report data from teachers regarding their professional development interactions and to supplement these data with classroom-based observations focused on the topic, or proposed result, of the professional development session.

There are numerous lists like Porter's (2003) published by organizations such as the American Federation of Teachers, Association for Supervision and Curriculum Development, Education Development Center, Education Research Service, National Staff Development Council, National Governors Association, National Institute for Science Education, and the U.S. Department of Education. As expected there are commonalities and differences among all the lists. One recent review of the research literature looked across 21 such lists that were part of studies that met the inclusion criteria of experimental or quasi-experimental research designs, match control groups, and good data measures (Larson, 2005). The purpose of this study was to identify the components of professional development models that have been proven effective through means of rigorous research. Table 6.3 lists the nine components of effective professional development that Larson's analysis identified.

These nine components represent a good starting point for efforts aimed at developing the quality of professional development experiences. By focusing on what works, or what is linked to school effectiveness, you can encourage professional development opportunities that empower teachers to make a positive impact on student performance (Larson, 2005).

Utilizing these nine components of effective professional development, you can create any number of mechanisms to help organize the collection and analysis of teacher professional development data. For example, you might create a template for each individual teacher, grade-level team, or departmental unit. Table 6.4 provides an example of what such a data collection instrument may look like. You will notice that the form includes a place for the teacher and leaders to discuss professional goals for the year. This will likely be linked to the mission and goals of the school, state and school standards for a particular content area, and perhaps teacher evaluation from a previous school year. The column on the focus of the professional development will allow school leaders and teachers to track what particular domains of classroom experience are being targeted, whether it is enhanced content knowledge (to help bolster low performance in a particular content domain from prior achievement test results) or pedagogical techniques that may have a broader application. The final column will allow you to collect data about the degree to which individual teachers, teams, and the whole school are taking part in professional development experiences that are aligned with effective professional development.

Table 6.3 Effective Professional Development Components and Corresponding Supporting Studies

Professional Development Components	Number of Supporting Experimental Studies (N = 7)	Number of Supporting Quasi-Experimental Studies (N = 14)	Total Number of Supporting Studies (N = 21)
Linked to Student Learning Outcomes	5	13	18
Job Embedded	5	13	18
Ongoing and Sustained, With Follow-Up	5	8	13
Incorporates Authentic, Active Learning Experiences	6	11	17
Includes Subject Matter Content	7	13	20
Encourages Reflection on Pedagogy, Content, and Beliefs	7	14	21
Incorporates Collaboration With Colleagues and/or Experts	5	12	17
Provides Support for Teachers	6	10	16
Measures Impact on Student Achievement	5	11	16

SOURCE: From Cavalluzzo, L., Lopez, D., Ross, J., Larson, M., with Miguel, M. (2005). *A Study of the Effectiveness and Cost of AEL's Online Professional Development Program in Reading in Tennessee.* Retrieved 2005, from http://www.ael.org. Copyright © 2005, Edvantia. Reprinted with permission.

Becoming a teacher is an ongoing process. Therefore, teachers must be equipped with the ability to reflect upon and learn from teaching (Darling-Hammond & Snyder, 2000). This process can be facilitated by thoughtful, integrated, and context-sensitive faculty evaluation and professional development systems (Darling-Hammond, Wise, & Klein, 1998). You play a key role in moving schools toward these coherent systems focused on improving the core technology of schools, namely, teaching and learning (Davis, Ellet, & Annunziata, 2003; Murphy, 1992).

Table 6.4 Professional Development Matrix

Teacher/ Team Member	Annual Professional Development Goals	Focus of Professional Development Activity	Correlates of Effective Professional Development
Smith	1. 2. 3.		__ Linked to Student Learning Outcomes __ Job Embedded __ Ongoing and Sustained, With Follow-Up __ Incorporates Authentic, Active Learning __ Includes Subject Matter Content __ Encourages Reflection __ Incorporates Collaboration w/Colleagues __ Measures Impact on Student Achievement
Jones	1. 2. 3.		__ Linked to Student Learning Outcomes __ Job Embedded __ Ongoing and Sustained, With Follow-Up __ Incorporates Authentic, Active Learning __ Includes Subject Matter Content __ Encourages Reflection __ Incorporates Collaboration w/Colleagues __ Measures Impact on Student Achievement
Rodriguez	1. 2. 3.		__ Linked to Student Learning Outcomes __ Job Embedded __ Ongoing and Sustained, With Follow-Up __ Incorporates Authentic, Active Learning __ Includes Subject-Matter Content __ Encourages Reflection __ Incorporates Collaboration w/Colleagues __ Measures Impact on Student Achievement
Chan	1. 2. 3.		__ Linked to Student Learning Outcomes __ Job Embedded __ Ongoing and Sustained, With Follow-Up __ Incorporates Authentic, Active Learning __ Includes Subject-Matter Content __ Encourages Reflection __ Incorporates Collaboration w/Colleagues __ Measures Impact on Student Achievement
Robinson	1. 2. 3.		__ Linked to Student Learning Outcomes __ Job Embedded __ Ongoing and Sustained, With Follow-Up __ Incorporates Authentic, Active Learning __ Includes Subject-Matter Content __ Encourages Reflection __ Incorporates Collaboration w/Colleagues __ Measures Impact on Student Achievement

The Professional Community of Teachers

The typical organization of schools and teachers' work allows teachers to work alone, isolated in separate classrooms most of the day. These arrangements provide limited time, and school budgets often provide slim resources for teachers to meet and talk together about how they can improve student learning. A professional community of teachers focuses on issues of teacher collaboration, teacher learning and professional development, expanded roles for teacher leadership, and the development of professional relationships among teachers (Bryk, Sebring, Kerbow, Rollow, & Easton, 1999).

What data can be used to measure professional community in school? As suggested earlier, a discussion with the faculty about what is meant by professional community is a first step. The types of data available to measure professional school community are similar to those for school climate, such as surveys, and observations.

Surveys as a Means of Measuring Professional Community

Numerous surveys ask teachers about their perceptions of the professional community in their schools. Examples are provided in Figures 6.4 and 6.5.

Figure 6.4 Professional Community Sample Survey

This school year, how often have you had conversations with colleagues about

a. What helps students learn the best

b. Development of new curriculum

c. The goals of this school

d. Managing classroom behavior

e. Content or performance standards

f. Instructional practices

g. Assessment of learning

Responses: *never, less than once a month, two or three times a month, once or twice a week, almost daily, does not apply.*

SOURCE: See, Study of Instructional Improvement, University of Michigan, School of Education.

Figure 6.5 Professional Community Survey Items

Please indicate the extent to which you agree or disagree with the following statements about the school in which you work. Mark (X) EACH item.	Strongly Disagree	Disagree	Agree	Strongly Disagree
Teachers at this school respect colleagues who are expert in their craft	☐	☐	☐	☐
Teachers in this school trust each other	☐	☐	☐	☐
Teachers in this school really care about each other	☐	☐	☐	☐
Teachers respect other teachers who take the lead in school improvement efforts	☐	☐	☐	☐
Many teachers openly express their professional views at faculty meetings	☐	☐	☐	☐
Teachers in this school are willing to question one another's views on issues of teaching and learning	☐	☐	☐	☐
We do a good job of talking through views, opinions, and values	☐	☐	☐	☐
Teachers are expected to continually learn and seek out new ideas In this school	☐	☐	☐	☐
Teachers are encouraged to experiment in their classrooms in this school	☐	☐	☐	☐
Teachers are encouraged to take risks in order to improve their teaching	☐	☐	☐	☐
Teachers in this school expect students to complete every assignment	☐	☐	☐	☐
Teachers in this school encourage students to keep trying even when the work is challenging	☐	☐	☐	☐
Teachers in this school set high expectations for academic work	☐	☐	☐	☐
Teachers in this school think it's important that all students do well in their classes	☐	☐	☐	☐

SOURCE: See, Study of Instructional Improvement, University of Michigan, School of Education.

A number of other aspects of professional community are key to the notion of a professional community that should be considered when collecting data. The nature of the relationships among teachers and formal and informal leaders and administrators in the school is central to a healthy learning community. Such items as "leaders and teachers collaborate to make this school run effectively" or "teachers feel respected by the school's leaders" are examples. Furthermore, this component addresses the extent to which leadership and expertise is distributed in the school. Do teachers ask other teachers for help? Do teachers confer with other teachers around instructional and subject matter questions?

Behaviors and Structural Arrangements

An important indicator of teacher professional community is the extent to which teachers actually do interact with each other around teaching and instruction. One type of data that helps illuminate these interactions is the schedule of teaching. A specific issue to asses is whether there is a scheduled common teacher planning time.

PARTNERSHIPS WITH PARENTS, FAMILIES, AND THE COMMUNITY

The term *community* is multifaceted and thus should lead to the collection of multiple types and sources of data to gauge the nature and extent of school-community relationships. One dimension of this relationship is parent and family involvement. Parent or family involvement can include school-based activities such as attending parent-teacher conferences and volunteering in the classroom, as well as home-based activities such as helping with homework, reading with the student at home, and talking about school matters. A large body of research links parent involvement to positive benefits for students, families, and schools, including academic achievement (see Epstein, Simon, & Salinas, 1997; Henderson & Mapp, 2002; Hoover-Dempsey & Sandler, 1997). Effective schools are characterized as providing opportunities for parents to both support and participate in their children's education (Mortimore, Sammons, Stoll, Lewis, & Ecob, 1980; Smith & O'Day, 1991). In turn, effective principals are those who bridge with the community to facilitate parent involvement. Principals are in a role to act as "environmental leaders operating in the community outside their schools while also bringing the community into their schools" (Goldring & Sullivan, 1996, p. 207).

Another dimension of school-community relationships goes beyond parents. Recent research suggests that the school community is much broader than guardians and parents. Educators have long argued that schools alone often lack the capacity to address the multiple challenges facing students in today's society, especially as pivotal indicators of social well-being continue to decline. Furthermore, recent learning theories suggest that communities can be much more closely connected to teaching and learning with the goal of linking in-school learning to real-world contexts in which such knowledge must be used (Wehlage, Newmann, & Secada, 1996). Productive school-community relationships can best be facilitated when educators better understand the nonschool environments in which students function (Bransford, Brown, Cocking, 2000). Communities not only provide the structures that facilitate learning but also shape and determine what learning is valued. Thus it is critical for education leaders to recognize and understand out-of-school contexts and the importance of the nonschool learning communities that shape students' understandings.

Measuring Parent Involvement and Satisfaction

Surveys

One way to collect data regarding parent involvement is to follow the survey procedures outlined earlier. Thus parents and community members can be surveyed about specific issues that are deemed important for your school-improvement efforts. Again we remind you that it is important to first have clarifying conversation about what is meant by parent and community relationships for your school. An example of school-community relationship survey data is provided in Figure 6.6.

Figure 6.6 The Relationship of Schools to Their Community
End of Year Data Collection

COMMUNITY COLLABORATION

GOAL: 95% of respondents to a family survey will indicate that they

1. Receive enough communication to be kept informed
   of school activities   93.7

2. Get adequate information about their child's progress
   between report cards   91.7

3. Feel free to express concerns or make suggestions   89.4

Based on these survey data, 93.7 percent of the families at this school indicate that they receive enough communication to be kept informed of school activities; 91.7 percent of the families get adequate information about their child's progress between report cards; and 89.4 percent report that they feel free to express concerns or make suggestions. The responses from the families are fairly high. For the school to meet the district goal, the school may want to address the ability of families to address their concerns or make suggestions to the school. Notice that these data are for only one school year. Thus if you had data for several years, you would be able to determine whether the school has made improvements on any of the same items.

Participation Data

One source of data often overlooked by schools is participation data. Participation data will allow you to access such questions as the following: How many parents attend parent-teacher conferences? How many parents and community members volunteer at school? Is there a small group volunteering over and over again, or is there a broad-based group of support? How often are community groups part of the teaching and learning in the school? To what extent are community members participating in our outreach programs such as parenting classes? To what extent do we as educators embrace the community as a resource for teaching and learning? Tracking this type of information over time, by grade level, and for each teacher is an important first step to understanding the extent of community and parent participation at school. It is important that the involvement go beyond symbolic ceremonies and that these events do not detract from the curriculum. The contribution of parent, family, and community involvement is when they are linked to the curriculum in the school.

Fortunately, these data are often routinely collected because visitors and volunteers are required to sign in at the office. However, if this valuable source of data is not viewed as data, it will go unnoticed and unused. Thus you must help the school determine who will be responsible for tallying up the volunteer sign-ups, as well as what other information your school wants from volunteers when they sign in. For example, the school may want to know what task they are going to do and what teacher they are going to work with.

Community Mapping

It is often helpful to think of a school's community in terms of three sets of resource categories: neighborhood economic and demographic attributes, neighborhood liabilities, and neighborhood assets. *Demographic data* about the school zone level can include such information as median household income, percentage of households in poverty, percentage unemployed, percentage on public assistance, percentage of children living in a single-parent household, percentage of housing units owned, number of public housing units, percentage of adults without a high school diploma, and percentage of adults with a bachelor's degree. These data are easily available from the U.S. Census Bureau (http://www.census.gov) and the local chamber of commerce.

Cognitive learning theory tells us that the construction of quality learning environments must include learner-centered and community-centered components. These components are part of the *How People Learn* framework (see Bransford, et al., 1999). Within this framework, the learner-centered component suggests that learning environments and experiences should draw up the existing knowledge, skills, dispositions, and cultural experiences of students. The community-centered component acknowledges that all learning takes place within the context of a broader social community that is linked through demographic characteristics. As such, local economic and demographic data help school leaders and teachers connect learning experiences to the contexts of the students' lives. Additionally, these data help school leaders think more strategically about meeting context-specific needs of students that arise from particular demographic and economic conditions.

Liability and Asset Data

Liabilities include teen births, drug arrests, weapons arrests, domestic violence arrests, and other crime incidents in the school zone. Assets include licensed child care programs, community centers, youth service organizations, churches, synagogues, hospitals, libraries, colleges and universities, and other community resources that are in close proximity to the school. Often this information is available through local municipality offices. However, if it is not readily available, or even if it is, nothing can replace getting out into the community to acquire firsthand knowledge of the school community. This can be facilitated by encouraging your faculty get out into the community and collect data by taking a "community walk." Getting to know central shop owners close to school can help establish a relationship with individuals and groups who can help be your eyes and ears in the community.

Figures 6.7 and 6.8 depict two community maps compiled with the information from city agencies. Figure 6.7 provides an aerial view of the many resources available within the community that can serve as assets to a child's education. For example, if your school library has limited holdings, you might form a partnership with the neighborhood library. If a group of students at your school would benefit from extended day programs, this type of arrangement could be pursued in partnership with the local YMCA, boys and girls clubs, before and after school care, and community centers. Within the Bass Middle School zone (see Figures 6.7 and 6.8), there exist 14 such organizations that may be able to assist school leaders with crafting a solution to providing a safe and educational experience for students before and after the normal school day.

Although there are many assets that exist within every school zone, there are also numerous liabilities. The liabilities within the Bass Middle School zone are provided in Figure 6.8. Benefiting from these data, your school community can be aware of pockets of competing forces surrounding the school and more able to provide appropriate interventions and programs addressing these social issues. For example, on the eastern edge of the Bass Middle School zone, a host of drug offenses has occurred. As such, a strategic school leader might plan several programs and interventions providing students with awareness of the negative impact of drugs and provide assistance for students whose daily life is impacted by such offenses.

Figure 6.7 Community Map of Resources for Children

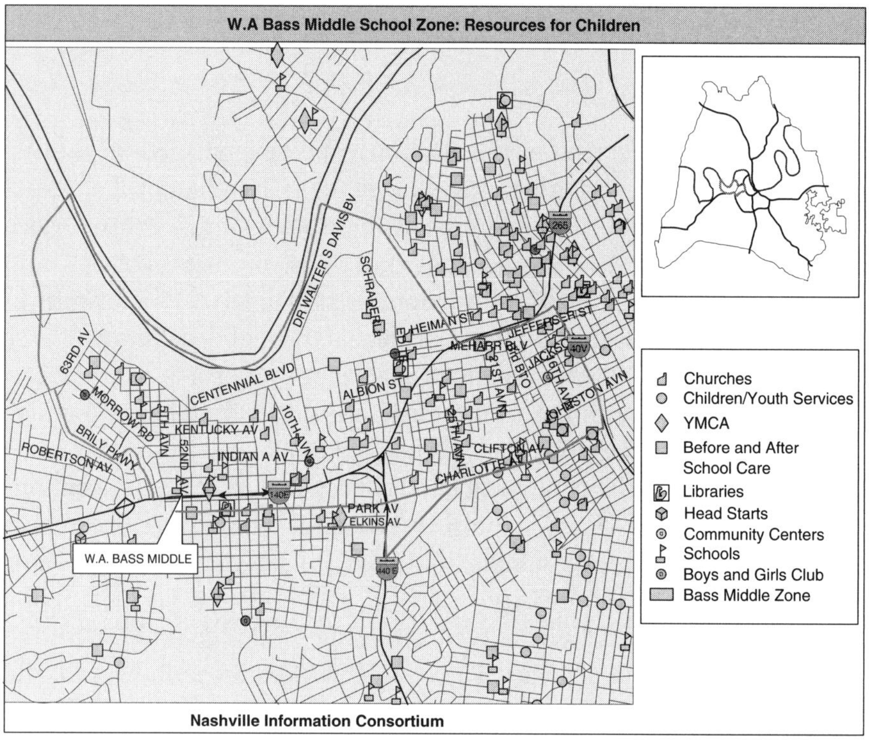

SOURCE: Based on statistics from NIC (Nashville Information Consortium).

Figure 6.8 Community Map of Liabilities Within School Zone

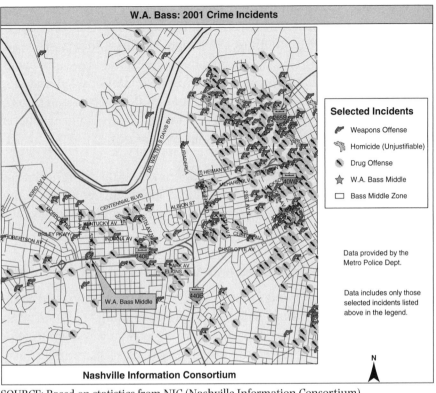

SOURCE: Based on statistics from NIC (Nashville Information Consortium).

CULTURE AND CLIMATE FOR STUDENT LEARNING

The most common definitions of school climate and school culture that supports student learning include key dimensions such as communication among staff, communication between staff and community, engagement in activities to support effective instruction and improved learning, and a safe and orderly environment where everyone can learn. Although here we will discuss these terms together, as parts of the same whole, there are distinctions between the two. For example, whereas *school culture* refers to the sum of the values, cultures, safety practices, and organizational structures within a school that cause it to function and react in particular ways, *school climate* refers mostly to the school's effects on students, whereas *school culture* refers more to the way teachers and other staff members work together (McBrien & Brandt, 1997). Positive school cultures contribute to the school's capacity to successfully implement high-quality reform strategies and interventions. Numerous types of data measure school climate; the most prevalent are survey questionnaires, classroom observations, and frequency of occurrences of specific behaviors.

It is important to set a measurable goal regarding school climate, but before a goal can be set, there must be agreement and shared understanding throughout the school community regarding what is meant by school climate and school culture. What kind of culture do we want at our school? What do we mean by a safe and orderly climate? A climate with mutual respect? A climate focused on learning for all? Consider analyzing discipline referral patterns on the student level. Does a particular group of students miss out on a significant amount of classroom instructional time based on the amount of time they spend waiting in the office to meet with a counselor?

These consensus-building conversations are important for using data because without shared understanding about why we are collecting and reporting the data that we are, the data will fall on the equivalent of unprepared soil.

Measuring School Climate and Culture With Surveys

Perhaps the easiest and fastest way to collect information about the school's climate and culture is through surveys. An initial question many educators ask is, do we need to write survey items or are there existing surveys available from other sources? In most cases there are numerous existing surveys that educators can use to assess school climate and culture. However, it is important to first clarify within your specific school community what domains and dimensions you wish to measure before using off-the-shelf items. This is important so you avoid using surveys simply because they are available. An obvious advantage of using available surveys is that often these surveys have been assessed for reliability and validity. In addition, depending on your school budget, you can contract with survey firms and developers to assist in collecting the data, analyzing the data, and providing the school with a comprehensive report. The report can often compare your school to schools with similar demographic characteristics and provide assistance in interpreting and implementing the results.

 Survey data should be collected from multiple stakeholders in the school: teachers, students, and parents, for example. This is important because survey data is based on respondents' perceptions, attitudes, and feelings. Just because students indicate they feel safe at school does not mean that teachers believe that all students are safe at school.

When collecting survey data from multiple stakeholder groups, give a large proportion of each group the opportunity to respond. For teachers the easier way to collect data is during a required faculty meeting, whereas student surveys can be collected during class time. The most difficult groups to collect information from are parents and community members. Information from the most vocal dissatisfied community members, or the most involved and supportive members only, would not provide a complete picture of parent and community members' perceptions of the school climate. Surveys can be collected through multiple avenues: at school events; sent home with the child, in the mail, or in a newsletter; or placed at community centers, libraries, and churches. Often incentives, such as a pizza party if 80 percent of the parents of a homeroom return the survey, are successful to rally responses. Survey data can provide information about how multiple stakeholder groups view the school on key pathways to school improvement.

Survey data can be collected on paper, via a Web-based instrument, or even through an interview. Survey responses are provided on a scale, with the resultant measurement being provided along a continuum in response to a statement. The most frequently used scale is the *Likert Scale*. Respondents indicate the option that most closely represents their feelings or opinions in response to a given statement. For example,

Do you feel safe at school?

Never   Rarely   Sometimes   Always
_____1   _____2   _____3   _____4

Often surveys use a two-point scale, providing just two responses such as *yes* and *no*.

Do you feel safe at school?

Yes_____ No_____

Although the two-point scale may be easier to use and faster to respond to, by eliminating the full range of responses, it often forces the respondent to take a position that is not necessarily reflective of his or her true feelings simply because there was not a range of alternatives given. Yet for younger students, the two-point scale may be more appropriate.

Results for attitude surveys are usually reported as the percentage of the responding group that felt a certain way. Alternatively, you can add the item scores from the response category (1–4) for the group of respondents (i.e., all students) to get a sum that indicates how positive the response is toward the statement being rated. If the question is a two-point scale, you can give a +1 to positive response (yes) and a zero or −1 to negative answers (no) and calculate a sum. If you ask parents, teachers, and students the same questions on the same scale, you can easily compare the responses from the various stakeholder groups.

It is important to collect responses to these types of questions at the same time each year to get an accurate assessment of change. As we know many factors can impact respondents' opinions and feelings, and by collecting data during the same time frame each year, you reduce outside factors that can impact responses (for example, the stress of starting a new school, new teachers who do not know that much about the school's culture, end-of-year testing anxiety, and so on).

In Figure 6.9 we present the results of part of a school climate survey regarding a safe and orderly environment.

Figure 6.9 Elementary School Climate Survey (Students)
Safe and Orderly Environment at the end of the School Year

GOAL: 95% of respondents on an annual student survey will indicate that they

1. Feel safe at school	57.8
2. Believe students are well behaved	94.4
3. Know the rules for appropriate behavior and consequences for any infraction	92.2

The district where this elementary school resides conducts annual student and family surveys regarding the safety and orderliness of the school environment. The school climate surveys are a part of the district's annual data-collection plan. The district would like to receive 95 percent support on each of the questions from all stakeholders. On the student survey, three questions are reported. The results confirmed that 57.8 percent of the students feel safe at the school; 94.4 percent of the students believe that students at the school are well behaved; and 92.2 percent of the students know the rules for appropriate behavior and consequences for any infraction. Clearly, the most striking response is that close to 43 percent of the students do not feel safe at the school, whereas 94.4 percent of the students believe that the students are well behaved. These data indicate that the students do not feel safe due to reasons other than student behavior. The administrators and teachers at this school may want to use this information to concentrate efforts on determining why the students do not feel safe.

Frequency of Behaviors

Data are routinely collected at school regarding discipline such as in- and out-of-school suspensions, office referrals, and types of infractions. These data can be tallied and graphed as important indicators of the school climate. Following is a graph of the number of office referrals for disruptive and violent behavior across four years. Figure 6.10 suggests that the climate is becoming more disruptive in the school as there are more office referrals each year.

Figure 6.10 Office Referrals for Disruptive and Violent Behavior

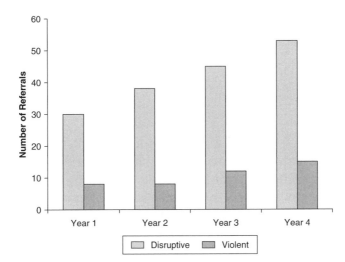

However, for us to better diagnose what is happening with discipline in the school, this graph raises a number of questions. For example: Is the increase in the number of office referrals a result of more students being sent to the office or the result of a small number of students being sent to the office numerous times? Are some teachers more likely to send students to the office than other teachers are? Ultimately, you will want to have a discussion throughout your school community about discipline policies. The first step is to dig deeper into the data and disaggregate it by teacher and students. In this way we are able to gain a deeper understanding about the issues of central importance to a positive school culture and climate.

Equally important, data provide an opportunity to have conversations with a broad community of stakeholders. For example, imagine after disaggregating the office referral data by teacher you found the following, as presented in Figure 6.11.

Figure 6.11 Office Referrals for Disruptive and Violent Behavior

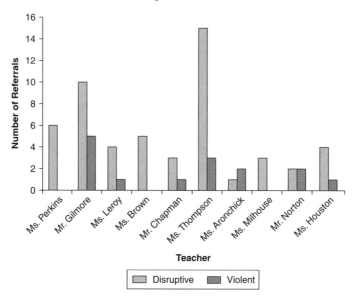

This disaggregated data would lead you to ask such questions as the following: Why is there such a difference among the teachers in the number and types of office referrals? Does the faculty have a uniform behavior system? Does the school need one? What is the goal in sending students to the office? Is it desirable to have misbehavior handled as much as possible in the classroom by the classroom teacher? It would also be helpful to disaggregate these data by the reporting categories required under No Child Left Behind to determine if certain students are more likely to be the subject of disciplinary actions by some teachers more than by other teachers. These types of questions can be the basis for careful deliberations among your school community to clarify policies, set goals, and monitor progress on one of the key pathways to school improvement and student achievement, namely, a safe an orderly learning environment.

RESOURCES ALIGNED TO GOALS

An important path to school improvement is to secure and allocate the appropriate and necessary resources to specific goals and targets of school improvement. Resources refer to money, people such as teachers and other personnel (counselors and tutors), and materials such as technology, supplies, books, and so on. Time is also a very important resource that is often overlooked. One important way to decipher the equitability of educational opportunity for all students is to assess the school budget. Are school-level resources being administered in a way that will ensure all students are able to meet high standards for performance? What disparities in opportunities to learn are brought to the surface when you analyze your school budget? When the resources that can facilitate student growth are passed out, are any pockets of students left behind? Are those students most at risk receiving the services and resources needed for their success? Such questions can be answered by analysis of existing school data. For example, look at the teaching schedules of your master teachers and those of your less experienced teachers. Do students of all ability and socioeconomic levels have equal access to the most effective instructors?

The data used in this pathway intersect with data from other pathways. For example, once professional development priorities are set, it is important to secure and allocate the necessary resources so teachers may participate in the appropriate learning opportunities. If technology is viewed as an avenue for improving student writing, but the appropriate software to help students write is not readily available on classroom computers, it would be important to allocate resources to both obtain the necessary software and ensure teachers are trained on how to incorporate computers into their instruction of writing narrative essays, for example.

Key questions addressed when using data to assess resources and their alignment to school goals are the following: Are all funds, regardless of source, allocated to meet both the school's student performance goals and needs of the professional learning community (such as high-quality professional development)? Are personnel effectively used to meet student performance goals? Does the structure of the day and the schedules support teacher and student learning goals? To address these types of questions a good place to start is to understand where your resources are currently used. Figure 6.12 is an example of a chart that Rosemont School uses to begin to analyze how much time teachers are spending on planning and whether they are planning together as teams or as individuals.

Teams of teachers can begin to collect data to address resource alignment questions as part of the problem-finding stage. Recall that involving groups of teachers is a core principle of data-based decision making. Teachers can address the following questions to bring back to the faculty: How are Title I and other external funds used within the school? How are specialists (counselors, coaches, tutors) used in the school? The answers to these questions should always be answered with specific data such as charts and tables. Figure 6.12 presents an example of a professional development audit that helps align professional development to goals and resources; Figure 6.13 provides an example of an aligned professional development plan and budget.

Figure 6.12 Example of Professional Development Audit

Elementary Teacher Time (Form 2T_E)

Description:
List the number of hours per grade/class that teachers spend on planning.

Goal:
Collect data on teacher planning time.

Column Description:
Content Area—Subject or grade.

Individual Hours—Amount of time that teachers at a grade level/content area spend on individual planning.

Team Hours—Amount of time that teachers at a grade level/content area spend planning with a team of teachers.

Total Hours—The program will add the individual and team hours columns.

Comments—Document any notable issues.

Content Area	Individual Hours	Team Hours	Total Hours	Comments
Kindergarten				
Grade 1				
Grade 2				
Grade 3				
Grade 4				
Grade 5				
Grade 6				
Grade 7				
Grade 8				
Special Education				
Art				
Music				
Physical Education				
Foreign Language				
Other				

SOURCE: Reallocating Resources for School Improvement: Analyzing Current Allocations, Center for Comprehensive School Reform and Improvement, Learning Points Associates. http://www.centerforcsri.org/pubs/reallocation/analysisforms.html

Figure 6.13 Example of Targeted Professional Development Plan and Budget

Professional Development Topic Activity	S.M.A.R.T. Goal Addressed	Date(s) and Times	Audience	Presenter	Budget: Dollar Amount and Source
Literacy					
24-Hour Training in Developing Literacy First	1A	Oct.–Dec. 2 strands 8:00–10:00 a.m.	Second cadre of teachers, K–Grade 3	Staff Developer/ Literacy Coordinator	$70,000 (Reading Excellence Grant)
24-Hour Training in Supporting Literacy	1A	3:30–5:30 p.m.	Second cadre, Grade 4–5	Consultant	$20,000 (Cohort IV funds)
Demonstration Lessons Coteaching Observation With feedback	1A	Sept.–June 9:30–3:30	Classroom teachers including teachers of bilingual and special needs learners	Staff Developer/ Literacy Coordinator Literacy Coach Consultant	$70,000 (see above) $14,000 (Cohort IV) $20,000 (see above)
Model Classrooms for Writers' Workshop	1A	Nov.–June (ongoing)	Classroom teachers	Joanne Hindley	$20,000 materials (Title I) $800–subs (Title I)

SOURCE: Mass Insight Education & Research Institute. (2007). *Building Block Initiatives* Retrieved 2007, from http://www.massinsight.org/initiatives/buildingblocks/search.aspx

CONCLUSION

While focusing on the key indicators of successful schools, this chapter has discussed various types and sources of data that address the key factors that help leaders propel teaching and learning in schools. The summary chart following presents the pathways to effective schools and sources of data for each pathway. Education leaders must rely heavily on ongoing analyses of these school-improvement indicators for both school-improvement planning and data-based decision making. In this chapter we provided practical examples of data collection aligned with each of the key pathways to school improvement and discussed ways of using data to benchmark and gauge how well your school is implementing the key pathways to successful schools. This chapter has suggested that when a school community collects and analyzes data about student outcomes and key pathways to those outcomes, a school community will be ready to set forth a plan for school improvement and be in a position to continuously monitor and evaluate progress toward the school's key goals.

Figure 6.14 Summary Chart of School Effectiveness Pathways Data Sources

Pathway to School Effectiveness	Illustrative Sources of Data
Shared mission and goals	• Constituent surveys regarding goal importance and achievement • Mission- and goal-specific quantitative measures such as attendance data, behavioral referrals, test scores, amount of parent involvement
Rigorous content standards for all students	• State, district, and local content standards • Curricular frameworks • Analysis of student placement into challenging courses, by ability, racial/ethnic groups, SES, etc. • Classroom observation and teacher evaluation data
Curricular and instructional coherence and alignment	• State, district, and local content standards • State, district, and local assessments • Curricular frameworks • Classroom observation and teacher evaluation data
Expert teachers supported by coherent, consistent professional development	• Characteristics and foci of individual professional development experiences • Schoolwide data regarding overall professional development system • Teacher participation in content and process-oriented professional development experiences • Degree of alignment between teacher goals/needs and professional development experiences
The professional community of teachers	• Teacher surveys • Teacher interviews • Teacher observation
Partnerships with parents, families, and the community	• Measures of in-school involvement of parents and community members • Measures of out-of-school involvement of parents and community members • Surveys of parent involvement and satisfaction • Mapping of community asset and liability data and other demographic indicators pertinent to schooling
Culture and climate for student learning	• Survey questionnaires administered to a broad base of school constituents • Classroom and school observations • Frequency and magnitude of specific behaviors such as analysis of student discipline referrals disaggregated by classroom/teacher/activity type

Discussion Questions

1. To what degree does your school collect and analyze data in addition to student achievement data?

2. Use Table 6.1 to do a preliminary assessment of your current school or district mission statement. Are there any key components of the mission statement that are stated in immeasurable terms? Are you surprised by the types of data that currently exist to assess the degree to which your mission statement is being implemented? How might you go about generating the types of data needed to supplement existing data?

3. Choose one of the pathways to effective schools and describe in detail what data you would propose to collect for this domain, in what ways it should be analyzed, and what specific benefits this information will add to your organization.

4. What community information would you as an educational leader benefit from knowing about your catchment area?

Section III

Analyzing Data for School

Improvement and Student Learning

Involving the Community in Data-Based Decision Making

Does parent and community involvement positively impact the academic experience of students and enhance student performance? Are there effective strategies for connecting schools, families, and communities to the benefit of students and society? In recent years much research and practical wisdom have endorsed the important role played by parent and community involvement in the academic lives of students. At the end of this chapter, you should be able to describe the benefits associated with involving communities in schools, understand how to develop collaborative community and family engagement, and be knowledgeable about the processes of involving the community in data-based decision making and collecting data about community engagement.

VIGNETTE REVISITED

Rosemont School has some community and parent support. The leadership team realizes that only a very small segment of each of these groups is engaged in the school. You know much more can be done to develop partnerships with community groups and parents. You want to also involve them in the actual data decision-making processes. You want to better understand the community, and you want them to really understand where the school is headed and how they can support their child's learning. You wonder: What does the research say about effective school-community partnerships? What types of partnerships can be established? You want to craft a more comprehensive approach to community and parent involvement at Rosemont through involving parents and other community members.

Beginning in 2001, the No Child Left Behind legislation signaled a clear commitment not only to enhanced school accountability and heightened performance expectations for all students but also to the important educational role played by families and communities. The NCLB legislation updated the existing federal Title I program by articulating expectations for schools and school districts in the realm of engaging families and communities. The National Center for Family and Community Connections with Schools (Henderson & Mapp, 2002) explains that all schools receiving Title I funds must abide by the following requirements:

- Develop a written parent involvement policy with parents and approved by parents. This policy must include how it will build the school's capacity to engage families, address barriers to their involvement, and coordinate parent involvement in other programs.
- Notify parents and the community about this policy in an understandable and uniform format.
- Use at least 1 percent of the school's Title I funds to develop a parent involvement program. The law defines parent involvement as activities that "improve student academic achievement and school performance."
- Describe and explain the school's curriculum, standards, and assessments.
- Develop a parent-school compact, or agreement, about how families and the school will collaborate to ensure children's progress.
- Give parents detailed information on student progress at the school.

Although this federal legislation highlights the fact that there are legal requirements regarding parental involvement in schooling, community involvement in education remains a recognized, but underused, resource (Hindman, Brown, & Rogers, 2005). It is essential that school leaders understand the important role played by community involvement in schooling. It is vital that principals be aware of strategies that can effectively connect schools, families, and communities. Additionally, school leaders must know how to collect data regarding parent and community opinions and views about their schools and how to engage them in data-based decision making. These topics are covered in this chapter.

THE IMPORTANCE AND IMPACT OF COMMUNITY INVOLVEMENT IN SCHOOLS

Parent and community involvement is one of several conditions associated with effective schools and improved student achievement, as outlined in Chapters 2 and 6. It is important to note that all family members—including parents, siblings, grandparents, aunts, uncles, and "fictive kin" who may be friends or neighbors—often contribute in significant ways to children's education and development (Henderson & Mapp, 2002) and can be considered part of the community of schools. This chapter focuses on community involvement, which in addition to family involvement, includes the neighborhood and places around the school; local residents who live in the area and may or may not have children in the school but have an interest in the school; and local groups such as businesses and churches based in the neighborhood.

To create the organizational conditions that foster community involvement, principals must understand the impact that community involvement can have upon the academic and social development of students. Many teachers and administrators are trained to see themselves as individual leaders of classrooms or schools with less attention given to the development of teamwork or collaborative ventures with parents, community partners, and others interested in students' success in school (Epstein & Sanders, 2006). It is becoming increasingly important to know how to communicate effectively with various school constituents, share ideas, solve problems, and work together with community members (Bryk & Schneider, 2002; Jones, 2003; Murphy, 2002; Pounder, Reitzug, & Young, 2002). This is important not only because of growing demographic and ethnic gaps between educators and their students but also because of the endorsed benefits of previous community involvement efforts.

Research has analyzed the impact of community involvement on students. Studies that have explored the relationship between community involvement and student performance use a number of indicators such as

- For young children: teacher ratings of school adjustment; vocabulary, reading, and language skills; and social and motor skills
- Academic indicators: report card grades; grade point averages; enrollment in advanced classes; promotion to the next grade; and standardized test scores
- Attendance data; discipline data; and participation in school clubs, sports, or other extracurricular activities

For example, Henderson and Mapp (2002) reviewed 50 empirical studies of the impact of community involvement on student achievement and found the following benefits to be associated with community involvement in schools:

- Higher grade point averages and scores on standardized tests or rating scales
- Enrollment in more challenging academic programs

- More classes passed and credits earned
- Better attendance
- Improved behavior at school and at home
- Better social skills and adaptation to school
- Graduate and go on to postsecondary education

In addition to these benefits, individual research teams have uncovered specific benefits of community involvement within specialized domains of schooling. For example, Ariaza (2004) found that school reform initiatives have greater chances of sticking when the community actively participates as an empowered change agent. In a longitudinal study on school attendance, several family-school-community partnership practices were associated with increases in daily attendance and decreases in chronic absenteeism (Epstein & Sheldon, 2002). In a study of school engagement among Latino youth in urban schools, the following were found to enhance school engagement: teacher support, friend support, parent support, neighborhood youth behavior, and neighborhood safety (Garcia-Reid, & Peterson, 2005). Data from 82 elementary schools in an urban area indicate that, after controlling for school characteristics, the degree to which schools were working to overcome challenges to family and community involvement predicted higher percentages of students scoring at or above satisfactory on state achievement tests. These findings should encourage school leaders to address obstacles to family and community involvement to realize the benefits of community partnerships for student academic performance (Sheldon, 2003). Additionally, findings suggest that subject-specific practices of school, family, and community partnerships may help educators improve students' mathematics achievement. For example, when controlling for prior levels of mathematics achievement, longitudinal analyses of elementary and secondary school data indicate that effective implementation of practices that encourage families to support their children's mathematics learning at home was associated with higher percentages of students who scored at or above proficiency on standardized mathematics achievement tests (Sheldon & Epstein, 2002).

The theoretical framework that guides most thinking and research in the realm of community involvement in education was articulated by Epstein (1995, 2001) as the *theory of overlapping spheres*. In this theory the home, school, and community environments are "spheres of influence" that impact student growth and achievement. A greater degree of alignment between the three spheres will result in layers of support working synergistically to enhance student development. Conversely, the spheres can be pushed apart when a gap exists between institutional policies and individual beliefs and practices. Ideally, there is a level of dynamic communication and collaboration among the three spheres that result in enhanced student achievement. This alignment is one of the many challenging tasks facing educational leaders. Strategies for enhancing this alignment by connecting schools, families, and communities will now be described.

Programs and Processes of Connecting Schools, Families, and Communities

In the previous section, we highlighted some of the research that supports the notion that programs and efforts to engage the community in the life of the school do make a difference, in multiple ways, in the lives of students. The research endorses the fact that workshops for parents on helping their children at home have been linked to higher reading and math scores, and students in schools with community partnership programs have made greater gains on state achievement tests. In this section we describe how schools and school leaders can go about forming these community involvement partnerships by highlighting existing effective approaches. While studying the impact of home-school-community partnerships on student achievement, Henderson and Mapp (2002) concluded that schools that succeed in engaging families from very diverse backgrounds share three key practices:

- Focus on building trusting collaborative relationships among teachers, families, and community members
- Recognize, respect, and address families' needs, as well as class and cultural differences
- Embrace a philosophy of partnership where power and responsibility are shared

After having synthesized the existing empirical studies in the realm of community engagement, Henderson and Mapp (2002) offered several specific suggestions regarding how schools and school leaders can engage communities for the purpose of enhancing student achievement. These suggestions include

- Adopt a family-school-community partnership policy. The philosophy behind it should see the total school community as committed to making sure that every student achieves at a high level and to working together to make it happen.
- Identify target areas of low achievement. Work with families and community members to design workshops and other activities to give them information about how to help students learn. Provide

materials for families to use at home, and get ideas about how to help their children learn at school.

- Offer professional development for school staff on working productively with families and community members. Invite families and community members to attend.

- Assess the current family-school-community involvement program to determine how it is linked to learning. Work with faculty and community constituents to create activities that will foster a learning community.

Hindman and colleagues (2005) contend that community involvement in education has increased in the previous two decades as schools have formed partnerships with citizens and local business to provide volunteers, conduct fundraising, and harness expertise to benefit students. These initiatives promote student achievement and have also been shown to help community members develop a sense of ownership in their schools. Research has found that when one seeks to involve community members in schools, it is important to tailor the specific message or request to the desired population. During this process schools and school leaders are also encouraged to identify potential barriers that could make community members reluctant to become involved (Hindman et al., 2005).

The Learning First Alliance (2005) conducted a study regarding how America's public schools can be promoted by the forging of relationships between key school constituents. Based on their research of successful family-school-community partnership approaches, the alliance has suggested the following approaches that school leaders can take to enhance the efficiency of their community engagement program:

- Describe how schools support parents' efforts to help children succeed. Help parents understand the curriculum and homework assignments. See that school meetings and events are scheduled at times that permit parents to attend, and then publicize these efforts to the parents and community.

- Create a family-school-community compact that spells out how you expect parents to support their children's education and what parents and community members should expect from the school.

- Work with parents to develop a list of volunteer activities by school level. Create a clear job description for each activity, and provide an expected time commitment. Post this information on the school Web site and publish it in the newsletters.

- Highlight and celebrate parent volunteers at meetings, in the newsletter, and on your Web site. Invite parents to share tips with you about how they support their children's education. Highlight the many ways that parents and community members serve as partners in children's education.

- Make it easy for community members to ask questions, broach concerns, and offer ideas.

The National Center for Family and Community Connections with Schools (Henderson & Mapp, 2002) has analyzed family-school-community partnership programs to determine best-practice insights. The authors have uncovered several key insights from across the existing literature base. They cite a study conducted by Sanders and Harvey (2000) that identified three key factors that contributed to successful community partnerships: the school's commitment to learning, the principal's support and vision for community involvement, and the school's willingness to engage in two-way communication with potential partners about their level and kind of involvement. One key issue in community engagement is how schools can best connect with families and community members from diverse cultural and class backgrounds. Related to Epstein's theory regarding spheres of influence, Lareau and Horvat (1999) found that the greater degree of alignment between white middle-class parents and schoolteachers enabled the white parents to work more easily with school staff than did parents from different ethnic or class backgrounds. Related to this, Scribner, Young, and Pedroza (1999) identified five best-practice strategies used by school staff in working collaboratively with Hispanic parents and community members. These are building on the cultural values of Hispanics, stressing personal contact, fostering two-way communication, creating a warm school environment, and facilitating structural accommodations for parent and community involvement. Whereas this study highlights the need for somewhat personalized approaches for meaningfully engaging certain constituent groups, several studies highlight the overarching need for schools and school leaders to ensure that partnership programs are integrated into a comprehensive approach to student achievement (Smrekar, Guthrie, Owens, & Sims, 2001; Wang, Oates, & Weishew, 1995). Effective programs to engage families and community embrace a philosophy of partnership where the responsibility for children's educational development is a collective enterprise among parents, school staff, and community members (Henderson & Mapp, 2002).

Thus far this section of the chapter has presented numerous strategies and insights for making successful connections with parents and community members and encouraging them to become more involved in the life of the school. In the next section we turn to process and data-based decision making that can help develop and support these programs and partnerships.

Collecting Data on Involving the Community

In Chapter 6 we provided an overview of how one might approach the collection of data pertinent to community demographics. For example, we provided examples of how a school leader could create community maps highlighting liabilities and assets that school constituents have to contend with on a daily basis. Here we will discuss how you might approach data collection pertinent to key steps in the community-engagement process.

Chadwick (2004) suggested an overarching approach to engaging community members that includes steps such as

- Framing the issue
- Understanding constituent perspectives
- Identifying constituent groups
- Developing strategies to encourage constituent action

To thoughtfully approach these four steps and conduct community engagement activities in a systematic manner, it is important to collect and analyze appropriate data.

Frame the Issue

The research contends that successful community-engagement activities have a clear focus. The focus should be rooted in the mission and goals of your school, as outlined in previous chapters. Although the ultimate goal of family-school-community engagement is enhanced student growth and achievement, there are many paths to this destination (Chadwick, 2004) and many ways families and communities can both support and enhance the mission of your school. For instance, think about involving community members in your school-improvement planning processes to understand the appropriate starting point for community engagement. Furthermore, during this process you can engage with their community constituencies to learn about their aspirations and needs. Once the school-improvement process has been conducted, you might then form a community-engagement planning team to distill from the strategic plan the best mechanism to draw upon community resources to assist in the attainment of the goals outlined in your school's strategic plan. What are community members passionate about? Where might they want to engage?

Although student growth and achievement are the ultimate goals, preliminary activities may have a variety of foci. One mechanism to obtain information from the community is a *SWOT analysis*. SWOT stands for *strengths*, *weaknesses*, *opportunities*, and *threats*, and it provides a process to collect data from groups to understand and examine the school's internal strengths and weaknesses, and its opportunities and threats, as it pertains to specific goals. It is a general tool designed to be used in the preliminary stages of decision making.

The leadership team can use a SWOT analysis with multiple groups, including teachers and students, but we provide an example of its use to gauge community input to develop a focus for community involvement. The first step is to be clear why you are inviting community groups to participate in a SWOT analysis. In this example the purpose of the SWOT analysis is to gather data and information from the community to establish a focus for its engagement and involvement in areas aligned and consistent with the overall school-improvement goals and processes and community members' interests and resources. Your objective is to learn about community perceptions of strengths, weaknesses, opportunities, and threats. The information can be gathered in a workshop-like setting where an atmosphere conducive to the free flow of ideas is developed free from blame. These workshops or meetings can take place over time and across the community in various locations so numerous groups can participate.

In the example in Figure 7.1, we see a number of emerging trends as articulated by community groups and parents when asked to think about the academic program at Rosemont School. Based on this information, specific issues can be framed that help the school build on its strengths, address the identified weaknesses, take advantage of key opportunities, and overcome recognized threats. The SWOT analysis can both focus and energize community groups and build consensus around partnerships and setting goals.

Figure 7.1 SWOT Analysis Template—The Academic Program at Rosemont School

Strengths	Weaknesses
1. Highly qualified teachers 2. Safe climate for learning 3. Good library	1. Inconsistent policies 2. Not enough communication 3. No supplementary curriculum materials
Opportunities	Threats
1. Teachers willing to collaborate 2. Afterschool programs	1. Lowering of academic standards 2. Declining student enrollment 3. Widening achievement gap

The SWOT analysis, although not completely filled out in Figure 7.1, suggests, for example, that teams of teachers (building on the opportunities of collaboration) can each begin to unpack policies and examine which ones seem inconsistent to parents (weaknesses); similarly, the group can look at strengths as avenues to address threats.

Understand Constituent Perspectives

To determine the appropriate community group to collaborate with on an initiative, or to gauge broader perspectives regarding school issues than can be ascertained in a SWOT analysis, other mechanisms can be used to collect information. As such, it is important that you be acquainted with some options for ascertaining public opinion. Even though there is a variety of mechanisms to attain public information, it is important to use approaches that are appropriate for answering the questions at hand. For example, to get a broad picture of how a community feels regarding school safety, you would not need to conduct phone interviews that are time and resource intensive but could instead hold an open forum to gather this information.

Opinion research comes in a variety of classifications based on the manner in which it is carried out (Gallagher, Bagin, & Moore, 2005). A few examples of how you can collect information regarding the opinions, attitude, and perspectives from your community will be briefly described.

Forums and conferences provide you with a rough but important measure of how the school community feels about particular topics and to discover areas of satisfaction and dissatisfaction. Often these forums allow school-based individuals or groups—school leadership, teachers, or students—to present a proposed initiative or solution to an issue. After the presentation, audience members are given an opportunity to express their opinions and ask questions about the topic. Often an attempt is made to summarize the tone of the meeting and to gather a measure of how the group as a whole felt about the particular topic. This information can be quite useful in helping your school to determine the best course of action. In addition, these forums provide very important avenues for you and others to really listen to the external communities.

Advisory committees are established with the intent of including a balanced representation of interests expressed within the broader community. Whereas a forum or conference can easily involve more than a hundred individuals, an advisory committee is comprised of a much more manageable number of community members. This benefit is balanced by the danger of assuming that the full spectrum of ideas and beliefs present in the broader community is adequately represented on the advisory committee. Even so, the inclusion of a cross-section of opinion from the broader community is a valuable asset to school-reform initiatives.

Public opinion surveys are mechanisms for identifying community priorities, attitudes, and opinions. As such, many schools utilize survey data to guide decision making and to justify such decisions and again to garner information to determine school-improvement processes. Of course, the manner in which the survey is designed, utilized, and analyzed will have important implications for how useful the results are to school leaders. As such, before sending a survey out to the school community, a school should give thought to the design of the questionnaire, the wording of the questions, interview protocols, sampling techniques, data analysis, and reporting and use of the results. The four most commonly used methods of gaining public opinion through survey techniques are the personal interview, the phone interview, the mailed questionnaire, and the drop-off/pick-up questionnaire. As technology continues to develop and become more widely used by all sectors of the community, two additional survey techniques are becoming more widely used. These are the automated telephone questionnaire and Internet surveying via e-mail or interactive Web sites.

When conducting surveys, you need to understand the strengths and limitations of various surveying techniques (Berends, 2006; Berends & Zottola, in press; Gallagher et al., 2005). Each technique has it advantages and disadvantages in terms of making it easy for participants to respond and gathering high-quality data. For example, personal interviews have the advantages of making it easier to obtain a high percentage of respondents completing the survey and ensuring that the survey items are appropriately understood by those answering the questions. The disadvantages include a greater cost of people going out to conduct the interviews, training of those administering the surveys, and gaining access to the desired respondents. By contrast surveys administered over the Internet are cheaper and faster, can be disseminated widely, and provide data online instantaneously for analysis. However, the disadvantages of Internet surveys include having a low response rate because people do not fill them out, maintaining the Web site for respondents, and making sure that the sample is not skewed because people need access to computers and the Internet (a problem in some high-poverty schools, for example).

Identify Constituent Groups

Once an issue has been framed and a proposed strategy has been articulated, the next step involves the identification of appropriate constituent groups to engage in the endeavor. Schools can collaborate with a broad range of community partners to implement activities that will enhance the local learning community and educational experience of students. In Figure 7.2, Sanders (2006) provides examples of this broad array of potential partners for school-community collaboration, beyond parents.

Figure 7.2 Prospective Partners for School-Community Collaboration

Community Partner Type	Specific Examples
Businesses/corporations	Local businesses, national corporations
Educational institutions	Colleges and universities, high schools, and other educational institutions
Heath care organizations	Hospitals, health care centers, health departments, foundations, and associations
Government and military agencies	Chamber of commerce, fire and police departments, city councils, and other local government agencies and departments
National service and volunteer organizations	Rotary club, Lions club, Kiwanis club, VISTA, YMCA, United Way, AmeriCorps, Urban League, etc.
Faith-based organizations	Churches, mosques, synagogues, other religious organizations, and charities
Senior citizen organizations	Nursing homes, senior volunteer and service organizations
Cultural and recreational institutions	Zoos, museums, libraries, recreational centers
Media organizations	Local newspapers, radio stations, public television, cable networks
Sports franchises and associations	Minor and major league sports teams, college sports teams and organizations
Other community organizations	Fraternities, sororities, foundations, neighborhood associations, alumni
Community individuals	Individual volunteers from the surrounding school community

SOURCE: Adapted from Sanders, M. (2006). *Building School-Community Partnerships: Collaboration for Student Success.* Thousand Oaks: CA: Corwin Press.

Develop Strategies to Encourage Constituent Action

Having acquired a base of insight regarding constituent perspectives in particular domains, your next step is to appropriately engage community members in strategies and actions related to current issues or challenges facing the school after the results of data collection have been presented in various forums. One approach to encourage community engagement and involvement might entail a movement of key school members out into the community (Chadwick, 2004). Although a limited number of community members may have the opportunity, or the luxury, of visiting the school campus on a given day, you can meet the community members where they are, outside the school environment. Businesses, community centers, and faith-based organizations are locations that can provide forums for you to begin to engage, or reconnect, community members with the life of the school. School personnel can visit in the community to engage members of the community or to tell the story of what is going on with the local public school system. Having made such good faith efforts to meet the community where they are, you might find that community members are more apt to see the value in becoming engaged in the local schools and more willing to support schools in terms of time, talent, and treasure. Aligned with this desire to bring community members into the school and to engage them more substantially in decisions impacting the instructional program and educational experiences provided to students, you may include community representatives in the process of data-driven decision making.

Involving the Parents and Community in Data-Based Decision Making

Thus far we have discussed the importance of school-family-community partnerships and mechanisms to involve them in the framing of school issues and participating in areas of need. As you and your school go through the processes of collecting and analyzing data on the various school pathways, parents and community stakeholders can be involved throughout the process. Parents have a role in collecting, analyzing, communicating, and using data (see www.parents4publicschools.com).

Collecting Data

Parents and community members can be important partners in collecting data for the school-improvement processes. For example, if the school-improvement team has decided to focus efforts on increasing attendance and truancy, parents and community members can help collect data. They can observe local neighborhood hangouts to see if students are frequenting stores, restaurants, and parks during school hours. They can visit local store clerks and interview them regarding students who may not be in school at particular times of the day. They can help conduct a telephone survey of parents to see if there are transportation issues or other barriers preventing their children from attending school or arriving on time. In this manner parents and community members are data gatherers.

It is always important to keep in mind the Family Educational Rights and Privacy Act (FERPA) when involving parents in data-based decision making. This act is a federal law that protects the privacy of student education records.

Analyzing Data

Some parents may have skills that can help the school-improvement team in analyzing data. Parents can work with others to organize and analyze the data to make it accessible to other parents as well as provide support to school personnel on the team. For example, one school-improvement team focused its efforts on examining trends in ACT test results over several years. The tests results were in a folder in the guidance office but were never reviewed for looking at trends across time. Two parents experienced in using Excel entered and compiled the data in a number of charts that became the basis of deliberations. Because of FERPA, the guidance counselor had to delete the identifying information from the test results and then gave them to the parents to enter into Excel. Clearly, the data presented in Figure 7.3 is beginning to tell an important story regarding the gaps in the school by ethnic groups, and this confirmed some of the impressions that were gathered in the SWOT analyses mentioned earlier.

Communicating About Data

Parents and other community members can help communicate the results of data-based decision making. Often they can play an important role in communicating data by helping to both create and advocate for clear and parent-friendly data presentations. As part of school-improvement teams, advisory groups, and sounding boards, parent and community members help other parents grasp the importance of the data in school improvement and help parents understand the strengths and weaknesses of their school.

Using Data

Parents and community members can use the data to help participate in school-improvement processes such as those outlined earlier. They may serve as tutors in targeted classrooms; they may help secure resources from community agencies; or they may help obtain needed supplementary materials. The data help determine specific needs, and parents and community members can see that their efforts are targeted to these needs. In addition, they can be involved in the follow-up processes used to determine if change and improvements are occurring. Equally important, parents have a role in supporting their own child's learning in response to data regarding their individual child. This is addressed in the next section.

Figure 7.3 Comparison of ACT Profiles for Year 1 and Year 3

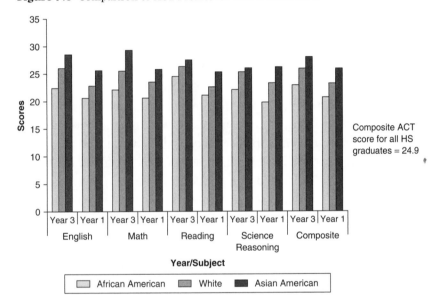

Helping Parents to Be Informed About School Data and Their Students

A very important role of the school leadership team is to help parents understand the school's accountability plan and to assist parents in interpreting information regarding their child's achievement. It is extremely important that parents understand the provision of the NCLB law and its annual testing requirements, as well as other aspects included under NCLB. Specifically, parents may have opportunities for supplementary services and school choices that require schools to communicate effectively with parents.

Helping Parents Interpret Standardized Achievement Test Scores and Other Information About Their Child's Learning

As partners in schooling, parents need to be informed about interpreting test scores. It is important to help parents understand that achievement tests are just one piece of information regarding their child's achievement.

Furthermore, parents should understand that the test score represents a snapshot from one time. If possible, it would be beneficial to help parents look at their child's test scores from several years to show how their child's performance has changed over time. Furthermore, there should be multiple forums and avenues of communication where it is explained how the school uses information from standardized tests to identify strengths and weaknesses in the school.

Beyond understanding achievement test results for their own child, parents should be informed about the progress of the school toward reaching its goals. The leadership team should present overall accountability information to parent groups regarding the school's performance over time. It is important to compare the school to other schools with similar demographics and to provide a breakdown by ethnic groups and socioeconomic level, which is consistent with NCLB.

School leaders can also help parents use other data about their child to get a complete picture about what their child is learning and how she or he is progressing. The goal is to help parents consider a variety of sources of data. Parents can learn how to examine their child's work and the teacher's assessment of it. Understanding their child's report card is another important course of information and data. As mentioned earlier, often student work is compiled in a portfolio. Parents should be informed about how students' work is aligned with local, district, and state standards.

Communicating Regarding Adequate Yearly Progress

Schools that do not show adequate yearly progress for all subgroups of students for two consecutive years and receive Title 1 funds are identified as "needing improvement" under NCLB. Parents must be informed that students in these schools are eligible to transfer to another public school, and the district must pay the transportation costs. The leadership team can play an important role in helping parents understand their options and helping them make the best decision for their child.

In addition, schools needing improvement must involve parents in the school-improvement process. The steps noted in the previous sections of this chapter can serve as a guide to developing partnerships to support the school-improvement process.

Furthermore, after a school's status of needing improvement continues, the parents are eligible for supplemental educational services such as tutoring and enrichment. This is a very important resource for the school, and once again the leadership team should take an active role in helping parents understand the opportunities and help them use data to carefully choose the services that will best help their child. Leaders and teachers should help service providers set goals for the student in partnership with the parents and regularly report the child's progress to both parents and teachers.

Communicating Strategies for School Improvement

Parents can best support their children's learning if they understand what they are being taught and how. Work with parents to organize a group that can be a regular part of your data-based deliberations and discussions. Communicating to a broad base of stakeholders about the purposes, results, and ongoing plans for data analysis is important for schools that want to sustain both improvement efforts and the community's involvement in those efforts.

Similar to communication about student progress and key school activities, communication about data-based findings should occur throughout the school year. It is not sufficient for stakeholders to receive sporadic or annual updates if an education leader hopes to encourage greater understanding of, support for, and involvement in data-driven decision making. Further, leadership teams should discuss which particular data-based updates could be disseminated without a conversation and which warrant an opportunity for stakeholders to dialogue about the results of data analysis. Such forums would provide an opportunity to discuss results, patterns, interpretations, and responses to trends illuminated by data. While affirming the school's commitment to the challenging process of utilizing data-driven decision making to enhance student performance, these efforts also endorse the commitment of school leaders to engage the community in meaningful dialogue.

CONCLUSION

Data can be an important lever for creating and sustaining community and parent involvement. Greater dialogue surrounding the collection and interpretation of data provides an opportunity to bridge the traditional divide that exists between the school and outside school communities; data can both help inform the school about community and family perspectives and needs and help the school best utilize community and family support and help. Gone are the days when schools serve just a subset of the population. As such, it is imperative that schools take efforts to broaden the scope of what and who counts within the educational community. The avenues for family and community engagement are many; the benefits are enormous. It is important to use systematic data-collection techniques throughout the processes. SWOT analyses and opinion surveys can help determine both areas of foci for community and parent engagement and their interests and capacity to address specific needs. Parents can be partners in the data-based decision-making process by being involved in each of the steps: collecting, analyzing, interpreting, and communicating. Lastly, leaders have a central role in helping parents understand and interpret the results of their own child's progress on achievement tests and other types of student work, as well as communicate widely the results of the school's efforts toward meeting its multiple goals, including its progress toward meeting adequate yearly progress under NCLB. These steps provide excellent opportunities to build a sense of community inclusive of the growing demographic diversity facing schools.

Discussion Questions

1. From your own experience, what are some of the most powerful benefits of family and community involvements in the educational experiences of students?

2. List several ways that community members are currently involved in the life of your school or district.

3. In what ways does your school leadership team currently engage community members in school decisions?

4. Describe the current degree of overlap between the *spheres of influence* in your school community. In what ways can you help to enhance the alignment among the home, school, and community environments?

5. Comment on the degree to which you think your school currently captures pertinent data on the various ethnic/racial/socioeconomic groups within your school community.

6. Describe a specific program you could initiate at your school that would engage a broad and diverse constituent base for enhancing student achievement.

7. Conduct a SWOT analysis, similar to the one offered in Figure 7.1, for the academic program in your school.

Analyzing Data
for School
Improvement

This chapter provides information about how to begin data analysis for school improvement. Where do you start? With all the data you have and all the data you want to collect, how do you begin to analyze the wide array of data? Based on the previous chapters, the school's mission provides a starting point. This chapter begins with an overall description of the school's achievement data and continues to describe the various ways data can be disaggregated to identify potential problems to address with various school-improvement strategies. The chapter also shows how different types of data might be used to further identify and focus school-improvement efforts. By the end of the chapter, you should be able to have a set of ideas about how you want to analyze your school's data in a number of ways to help your school community focus on a particular challenge of your school.

VIGNETTE REVISITED

You have examined Rosemont School's mission. You have compiled the data you have and collected the data you need to see if the school is fulfilling its mission. You have done this with your school data team and engaged the community in the ongoing processes of data-based decision making. Now what? It's time to begin to analyze the data. Where to begin? What will you analyze? How? As you assemble your data team, you all agree that it is important to understand how well your school is doing in fulfilling Rosemont's mission "to provide opportunities for all students to perform at or above grade level in reading, writing, and mathematics." Your leadership team decides to begin with getting an overall picture of Rosemont students' achievement, both with state assessment data and formative assessments. The journey continues as you peel the onion in different ways to better understand your school's strengths, weaknesses, opportunities, and threats so that your school can better focus its school-improvement efforts.

Up to this point, we have pointed the way toward using data for making decisions to improve your school. We have discussed the reasons for using data; the background for what it takes to lead successful schools; the pathways for school improvement; using standardized achievement scores, formative assessments, and additional data to measure pathways to student learning; and the importance of involving the community in the data-based decision-making processes.

In this chapter we provide examples of how to analyze the data you have collected and compiled to measure your mission. We focus on some of the descriptive analyses that are possible to examine part of the school mission. Remember Rosemont's mission? *The mission of Rosemont School is to provide a safe and secure environment and provide opportunities for all students to perform at or above grade level in reading, writing, and mathematics while demonstrating responsibility and self-control.* In this chapter we will focus on how well Rosemont is doing in terms of providing opportunities for students to perform at or above grade level in reading, writing, and mathematics. Because we have argued that state assessment scores are not the only indicators for understanding this part of the mission, we will also focus on formative assessments and some of the other data collected to understand this important aspect of Rosemont's mission.

The analyses that follow are descriptive only. Conducting multivariate or more sophisticated statistical analyses is beyond the scope of this book. In pointing the way toward a variety of ways to analyze data to describe Rosemont School, we hope to provide a heuristic for you as you engage in analyzing data for your school to identify strengths, weaknesses, opportunities, and threats.

Although the analyses that follow provide an example of identifying a problem in Rosemont to focus school-improvement efforts, the descriptive analyses cannot be seen as pointing to the *causes* of the problem. Such analyses require much more sophisticated methods, again beyond the scope of our purposes here and described more in the next chapter. Yet we believe descriptive analyses can be important. Using a wide array of data from your school can help your school community focus your school-improvement efforts so that you can better fulfill your school's mission. So let's get started. How well is Rosemont doing in terms of standardized achievement scores on state assessments?

STATE ASSESSMENT SCORES

The tables and graphs that follow are based on the overall achievement scores in reading, writing, and mathematics of Rosemont students over the past three school years. There are proficiency levels the state provides, ranging from Level I, the lowest level of proficiency, to Level IV, the most advanced level of proficiency. In Table 8.1 and Figure 8.1, we see that over the past three school years the percentage of students scoring in the proficient categories (Levels III and IV) has increased. For instance, the percentage of students scoring in Level IV has increased from 8 percent in Year 1 to 15 percent in Year 3. We see that the percentage of students scoring in Levels III and IV has increased from 62 percent in Year 1 to 71 percent in Year 3. Although not shown here, the leadership team of Rosemont finds that similar patterns exist for writing.

Table 8.1 Rosemont Reading Proficiency Scores on State Assessment Over the Past Three School Years

	Year 1	Year 2	Year 3
Level I	10%	5%	5%
Level II	28%	31%	24%
Level III	54%	53%	56%
Level IV	8%	11%	15%

Figure 8.1 Rosemont Reading Proficiency Scores on State Assessment Over the Past Three School Years

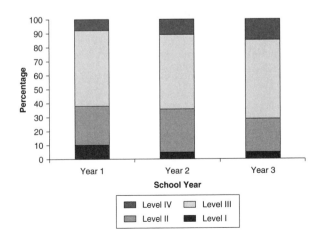

In mathematics Rosemont's overall scores tell a different story. When examining the overall mathematics scores in Table 8.2 and Figure 8.2, we see that the percentage of students scoring in the highest mathematics proficiency categories has decreased, and the percentage of students scoring in the lowest proficiency categories has increased. In Year 1, 7 percent of Rosemont students were scoring at the lowest proficiency level, and in Year 3, there were 12 percent of students scoring at this lowest proficiency level. Over the past three years, there was also an increase in the percentage of students scoring in Level II, the second lowest proficiency level. As the percentage of students in the lowest proficiency categories increased, the percentage of students in the highest categories decreased from 71 percent of students scoring in Levels III and IV in Year 1 to 55 percent in Year 3.

Something troubling appears to have been going on in mathematics over the past compared with what has occurred in reading and writing. But what?

The previous graphs should raise additional questions. For instance, school scores may change over time for a host of reasons. For example, student mobility in and out of the school may have an impact on overall scores. So, too, changes in the state cut scores for the proficiency levels may change over time. In addition, changes in school demographics such as increases in the number of students living in poverty may have an influence on changes in scores.

The data team examined these issues with the data they have. The team found that the cut scores on the state assessments have remained the same over the past three years. In addition, the team compared the scores of the students who moved out of the school to those who came in and found that these student groups were comparable in terms of their reading, writing, and mathematics scores. Finally, after examining the student demographic information for the school, the team found that the school's demographic composition has remained stable over time.

Table 8.2 Rosemont Mathematics Proficiency Scores on State Assessment Over the Past Three School Years

	Year 1	Year 2	Year 3
Level I	7%	8%	12%
Level II	22%	29%	33%
Level III	62%	54%	47%
Level IV	9%	9%	8%

Figure 8.2 Rosemont Mathematics Proficiency Score on State Assessment Over the Past Three School Years

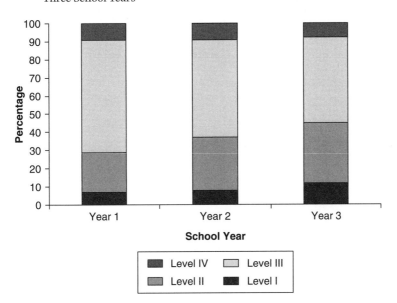

After examining these overall state assessment scores for Rosemont, the team continued to peel the onion. That is, they wanted to disaggregate the scores in different ways to better understand what is going on in reading, writing, and mathematics. Although the team generated a number of analyses, we present here some of their analyses in mathematics because the school scores suggest a decrease over time.

A couple of the team members took on the task of disaggregating the mathematics scores (other team members examined the other subject areas). First, these team members looked at mathematics scores by grade level over time. Their results appear in Table 8.3 and Figure 8.3.

Although there are a lot of numbers and graphs to look at for Rosemont, which includes multiple grade levels, the team takes time to examine what is happening in each grade across the last three years. Something appears to be going on in the lower grade levels compared with the higher grade levels.

For example, looking at either the specific numbers in Table 8.3 or the bar graphs in Figure 8.3, the patterns suggest that in Grades 6–8 there seems to be stability in the percentages of students scoring in the highest two categories of proficiency. Overall across Grades 6–8 across the last three school years, roughly 70 percent of the students are scoring in Levels III and IV.

Table 8.3 Rosemont Mathematics Proficiency Scores on State Assessment Over the Past Three School Years by Grade Level

Mathematics by Grade Level Year 1						
	Grade 3	**Grade 4**	**Grade 5**	**Grade 6**	**Grade 7**	**Grade 8**
Level I	6%	9%	8%	7%	6%	8%
Level II	20%	24%	22%	19%	20%	24%
Level III	63%	59%	64%	63%	58%	65%
Level IV	11%	8%	6%	11%	16%	3%
Mathematics by Grade Level Year 2						
	Grade 3	**Grade 4**	**Grade 5**	**Grade 6**	**Grade 7**	**Grade 8**
Level I	6%	8%	11%	8%	6%	9%
Level II	33%	35%	34%	27%	24%	23%
Level III	52%	50%	47%	52%	59%	61%
Level IV	9%	7%	8%	13%	11%	7%
Mathematics by Grade Level Year 3						
	Grade 3	**Grade 4**	**Grade 5**	**Grade 6**	**Grade 7**	**Grade 8**
Level I	14%	17%	16%	9%	8%	8%
Level II	41%	43%	40%	27%	23%	24%
Level III	38%	36%	36%	54%	56%	60%
Level IV	7%	4%	8%	10%	13%	8%

Although there may be a need to improve the percentage of students scoring in these higher proficiency categories in Grades 6–8, the data team notices something more troubling about what is going on in the earlier grade levels.

In the past three years, the percentage of third, fourth, and fifth graders scoring in the lowest proficiency categories has increased over time. For instance, looking at Figure 8.3 and following the bar graphs for Grade 3 down the page, we can see a pattern that about 25 percent of third graders scored in the lowest proficiency categories in Year 1 compared with about 55 percent in Year 3.

Figure 8.3 Rosemont Mathematics Proficiency Scores on State Assessment Over the Past Three School Years by Grade Level

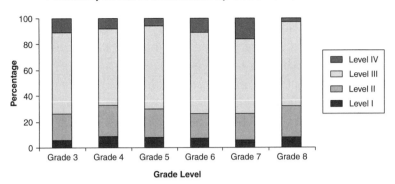

Percentage of Rosemont School Students Scoring at Different Proficiency Levels in Mathematics by Grade Level, Year 1

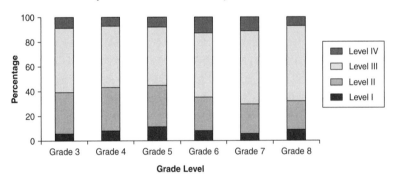

Percentage of Rosemont School Students Scoring at Different Proficiency Levels in Mathematics by Grade Level, Year 2

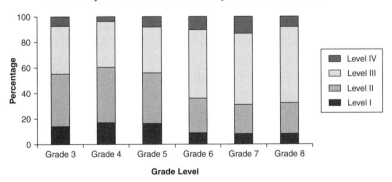

Percentage of Rosemont School Students Scoring at Different Proficiency Levels in Mathematics by Grade Level, Year 3

Similar patterns are apparent for fourth and fifth graders in that increasing percentages of these students are scoring in the lowest proficiency categories over time. In fact, the pattern seems even more troubling for Grades 4 and 5. For example, we see that 33 percent of fourth graders scored in Levels I and II in Year 1, and the percentage increased to 60 percent in Year 3. Similarly, the percentage of low-scoring fifth graders increased from 30 percent to 56 percent over this same time period.

What might be going on in the lower grade levels? These results provided Rosemont's leadership team with important results but raised more questions. How might they further examine the data to help pinpoint what is going on in these grade levels?

The data team did a number of additional analyses. The team disaggregated these grade-level data by gender, by race-ethnicity, by socio-economic status of the students, by whether the students were eligible for special education services, and by English language learner status. Although these results (not shown here) were helpful in seeing some important achievement gaps the school needs to attend to, the results revealed no changes in the gaps over time in ways that suggested that different student groups were driving the pattern of grade-level results the team found in the lower grade levels.

After all these analyses, questions still remained about what is going on with Rosemont students' mathematics scores. What else could be going on that related to the increased number of lower grade-level students scoring in the lowest proficiency categories on the state assessment?

The data team decides to examine a couple cohorts of students as they move across grades. Based on the scores they have in Year 3, the leadership team looks at the fifth graders and at their scores the previous two years back to Year 1. They do the same for the sixth graders and seventh graders in Year 3 to examine what patterns emerge for the different cohorts over their time at Rosemont.

A pattern does seem to emerge when looking at mathematics results across the three student cohorts. A substantial percentage of students is proficient in third grade, but then scores decline in fourth and fifth grades before improving again in sixth grade (see Table 8.4 and Figure 8.4). For example, in the first set of results for a cohort of students tracked from third through fifth grades, we see that about 67 percent of students scored in Level III and IV as third graders, but when this cohort moved to fourth grade, only 48 percent scored in the higher proficiency categories. In fifth grade the students scored only 44 percent at the higher proficiency levels.

A similar pattern emerges when looking at the other cohorts. For the cohort of students the data team was able to follow between third and seventh grades, we see that students scoring at the lowest proficiency levels increased in fourth and fifth grades compared with when the students were in third grade. When the students moved into sixth and seventh grades, the percentage of students score in Levels I and II declined.

Table 8.4 Rosemont Mathematics Proficiency Scores on State Assessment for Different Student Cohorts

Cohort Analysis: Third Graders in Year 1 Through Fifth Grade Year 3				
	Grade 3	**Grade 4**	**Grade 5**	
Level I	8%	15%	16%	
Level II	25%	37%	40%	
Level III	47%	39%	36%	
Level IV	20%	9%	8%	
Cohort Analysis: Sixth Graders in Year 3 Back to When They Were Third Graders				
	Grade 3	**Grade 4**	**Grade 5**	**Grade 6**
Level I	6%	16%	15%	9%
Level II	27%	42%	40%	27%
Level III	43%	33%	35%	54%
Level IV	24%	9%	10%	10%

Cohort Analysis: Seventh Graders in Year 3 Back to When They Were Third Graders					
	Grade 3	**Grade 4**	**Grade 5**	**Grade 6**	**Grade 7**
Level I	8%	20%	18%	11%	8%
Level II	28%	41%	39%	28%	23%
Level III	44%	33%	34%	46%	56%
Level IV	20%	6%	9%	15%	13%

What might be going on in the fourth and fifth grades? What else might the data team examine? What additional layers of the onion might they peel away? How might they better identify the problem in mathematics achievement for Rosemont students, particularly in the fourth and fifth grades?

The data team wanted to know more about what areas of mathematics were posing the most challenges to fourth and fifth graders. Thus they disaggregated the state assessment scores by mathematics performance domains and focused on the percentage of students who scored in the lower proficiency levels (Levels I and II). Figure 8.5 disaggregates the mathematics scores by different areas of mathematics assessed over the past three years.

The data team noticed that greater percentages of fourth and fifth graders scored in the lower proficiency categories in the areas of computation and real-world problem solving. For instance, in Year 3 nearly 60 percent of fourth graders and almost 70 percent of fifth graders scored in the lower proficiency levels on the computation part of the mathematics state assessment. In the area of real-world problem solving, 52 percent of fourth graders and 77 percent of fifth graders had scores in the lower proficiency levels.

Figure 8.4 Rosemont Mathematics Proficiency Scores on State Assessment for Different Student Cohorts

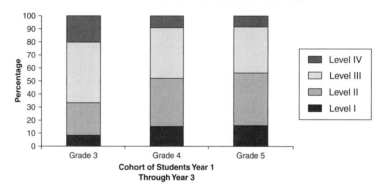

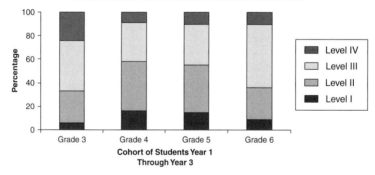

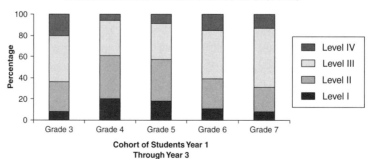

Figure 8.5 Rosemont Mathematics Proficiency Scores by Performance Domains

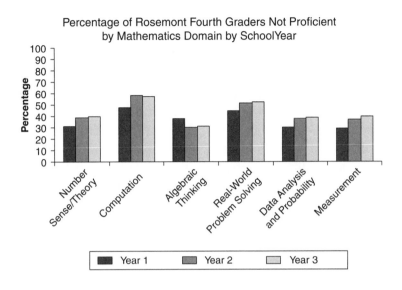

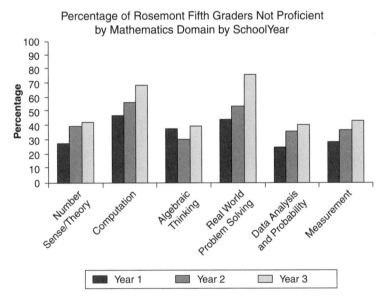

Formative Assessments

These results provided information to help focus the data team and the school on specific areas of mathematics. Yet the data team wondered how these state assessment scores related to the formative assessments that students took in the fall and spring to prepare them for the state test.

The formative assessment tests students in the same domains as the state assessment, so the data team examined the scores by domain for the students in their school. There were some interesting parallels, particularly in the fourth and fifth grades. Figure 8.6 shows the most recent scale scores for the fourth and fifth grades in the spring. There are some striking similarities between the scores on the state assessment and the formative assessment. The formative assessment scores also show that fourth- and fifth-grade students are scoring lower on those parts of the mathematics assessment that address computation and real-world problem solving.

The data team pressed onward. They were curious about how the state proficiency scores differed by teachers, so they disaggregated the scores by teachers and grade level. The data team was sensitive not to name teachers. An example of what they found for fourth-grade teachers appears in Figure 8.7, which shows the percentages of students in the lowest proficiency levels by teacher over the past three school years. The data team noticed that although there was an increase across all the teachers in the percentage of students scoring in the lowest proficiency categories, Teacher 2 seemed to face particular challenges regarding students' mathematics achievement. On the most recent mathematics test, 70 percent of Teacher 2's students were scoring in the lowest proficiency levels.

What else might be going on with teachers, particularly the fourth- and fifth-grade teachers who teach mathematics?

Figure 8.6 Rosemont Mathematics Scores on the Formative Assessment in Spring

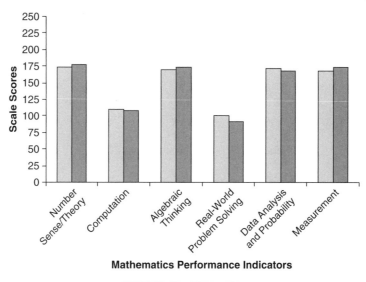

Figure 8.7 Rosemont State Mathematics Scores by Teacher

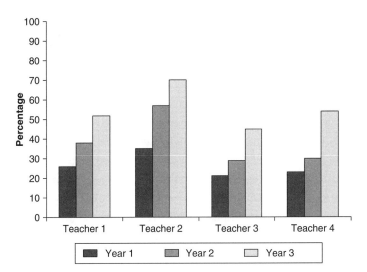

Additional Sources of Data

To examine what else might be going on in the school, the data team turned to data gathered through teacher surveys about some of the important pathways for school improvement. A set of questions on this survey asked the teachers to think about all the different professional development activities they participated in during the last 12 months. Teachers then reported the overall number of hours across all professional development activities; they also reported the number of hours that focused on reading/language arts and mathematics instruction. The data team's results are reported in Figure 8.8.

Figure 8.8 Professional Development of Rosemont Teachers
Over the Past Three School Years

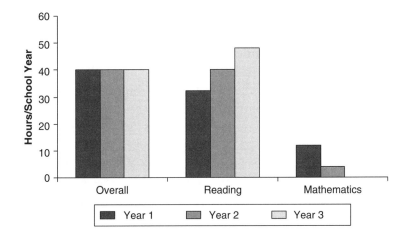

A couple of things struck the data team when they examined this chart. First, the overall level of professional development was the same over the past three years. Second, teachers' professional development at Rosemont increased steadily in the area of reading. Finally, professional development in mathematics decreased to the point where there was no professional development in mathematics in Year 3.

The data team also examined the overall experience levels of Rosemont teachers. When examining the average years of experience for the teachers, they found that the average experience in the last three years went down from more than 16 years in Year 1 to less than 14 years in Year 3. Although this decrease in experience over the past couple years is not striking, the data team wondered how teaching experience broke down by grade level. The results appear in Figure 8.9, which shows the average years of teaching experience overall and by grade level.

Figure 8.9 Teaching Experience of Rosemont Teachers by Grade Level

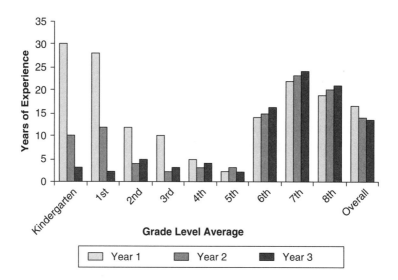

When the data team examined these results, the team noticed that the teaching experience is remarkably lower in the K–5 levels, compared with Grades 6–8. One of the teachers on the data team, who had been at the school for over 20 years, commented that some of the early-grade levels had experienced new hires over the past few years due to retirements.

With the inexperience of the lower grade levels, the lower mathematics achievement that is going on in Grades 4 and 5, and the lack of any professional development, the data team started to see some issues emerging that were worthy of focusing school-improvement efforts. However, they would have never been able to pinpoint these issues had they not examined the data in a number of different ways. Peeling the onion seemed to be working.

Yet the data team wasn't done. In addition to these instructional pathways, the data team had information about what was going on in their students' homes that supported achievement in school. Through surveys of both teachers and parents, they had data on the same issues (or survey indicators) from two different sources. Although based on parents' and teachers' perceptions, the questions on the surveys allowed the data team to get a sense of parent involvement in their children's schooling.

One set of questions of parents and teachers asked how frequently Rosemont teachers asked parents to engage in activities that supported their child's learning, such as attending to completion of homework by signing off, engaging directly in helping their child with homework, seeing excellent examples of high-quality work, and discussing student placements for instructional purposes. Teachers and parents could respond to the items on the survey by reporting, "never," "rarely," "occasionally," "fairly often," or "often."

Although the data team was careful to examine all the responses to these items for both parents and teachers, they decided to report to their school community only the percentage that reported "fairly often" or "often" because they felt that these results captured the key message and could be presented in a parsimonious, clear way. These results appear in Table 8.5.

Table 8.5 Percentage of Parents and Teachers Reporting That Rosemont "Fairly Often" or "Often" Engages Parents in Activities That Support Student Learning

	Parent Surveys	Teacher Surveys
Teachers require students to have their parents sign off on homework	2%	3%
Teachers assign homework that requires direct parent involvement or participation	5%	4%
Teachers send home examples of excellent student work to serve as a model	1%	2%
Teachers discuss with parents their child's placement in a particular instructional group or class	33%	40%

The overall message from this table of results is that both parents and teachers report that very few of these parent involvement activities were occurring. For instance, only 2 percent of the parents and 3 percent of the teachers reported that teachers require students to sign off on their homework. Only 1 percent of parents and 2 percent of teachers reported that Rosemont teachers send home examples of excellent student work to serve as a model. A greater percentage of parents and teachers reported that teachers discuss instructional groupings with parents, but given the importance of instruction in student learning, these percentages of 40 percent or less struck the data team as very low.

The data team also examined data from parent and teacher surveys (Table 8.6) that asked them to estimate the percentage of parents involved in different activities that aimed to build the school community and bring people together (e.g., parent-teacher associations, back-to-school nights, parent-teacher conferences, performances, and athletic events).

When examining these indicators of parent involvement, the data team was surprised again about how low the levels of parent involvement were at Rosemont. For example, parents reported that only about 10 percent of the school community was involved in the parent-teacher association, and teachers reported only about 8 percent. Although not exactly the same, both parents and teachers reported a small percentage of the overall Rosemont community is involved in the school's PTO.

Across all the activities, except one, parents and teachers agreed in their perception: The percentage of parents involved in different Rosemont community events was surprisingly low. It appears that the only Rosemont school activity that brought a substantial percentage of the community together was athletic events.

In addition to the academic issues of low mathematics achievement in the elementary grades (especially fourth and fifth) and inexperienced teachers in these grades who have received no professional development in mathematics instruction, the data team was able to further identify the challenge that parent involvement was very low throughout their school.

Having gone through so many sources of data linked to their school's mission, the data team feels as though it has arrived at some important issues that Rosemont needs to address. The team has analyzed the data, peeled the onion in a myriad of ways, and helped to identify some problems. Team members feel as though they have set some priorities for improvement that they would not have known about had they not examined the data. Yet some questions remain. What do they do now? Although they have identified some problems to focus school-improvement efforts at Rosemont, what strategies or interventions should they implement? How do they know a program or instructional strategy is any good? It is to these questions that we turn in the next chapter.

Table 8.6 Percentage of Parents Participating in School Activities as Reported by Parents and by Teachers

	Parent Surveys	Teacher Surveys
Parent-teacher association/organization (PTA or PTO)	10%	8%
Open house, back-to-school night	12%	11%
Academically focused events (e.g., science or math nights)	5%	2%
Parent-teacher conferences	9%	6%
Education programs for parents (e.g., family literacy, homework support workshops)	3%	4%
School performances	10%	11%
Athletic events	76%	80%
Volunteering in the school	13%	9%

Discussion Questions

1. Why did the Rosemont data team focus on standardized achievement scores to begin their analyses? What other achievement data did the team analyze and why? What data would your school's data team focus on first and why?

2. In what ways did the data team peel the onion when examining student achievement data? How might you peel the onion to help identify strengths and weaknesses in your school?

3. What other data did the data team analyze? How did analyses of these data help further identify problems in Rosemont? What other data would have been helpful to examine?

4. When you think of all the data on your school that helps monitor your school's mission, what plan would you set in place to organize the data team's analyses? What plan would you put in place to discuss results with the data team and the broader school community?

Section IV

Using Data for Decision Making

Seeking Solutions

9

Evidenced–Based Decisions

and Processes

This chapter focuses on making decisions about what to do when data help identify challenges in your school. However, the school data will take school improvement only so far. If mathematics instruction needs to be strengthened, how will the leadership team know what to do? This chapter sets out criteria for choosing an educational intervention. Moreover, it describes a process for considering solutions through addressing the following questions: Why is scientifically based research so important? What does the research say? How do leaders know which research to look at? What are other educators and schools doing? What are promising practices? What decision models can be used to set forth a path of implementation and change? How does the school monitor and evaluate their implementation strategy?

VIGNETTE REVISITED

The leadership team at Rosemont School has worked diligently to help teachers and the community understand why data-based decision making is so important. The team has made great progress in using data to focus priorities and interpreting and analyzing the data. At this point the team has identified specific pathways and challenges that need to be addressed. In fact, the

---

data helped find the problems and identify and prioritize their needs. The leadership team has learned, for example, that there is insufficient parent involvement in fourth grade, and fourth- and fifth-grade math achievement provides a significant challenge. The data have revealed that the most highly qualified teachers are all in the upper grades, whereas there are many newer, inexperienced teachers in the lower grades. However, the data do not usually help identify solutions or interventions for addressing the problems. The team now turns to making decisions about how to address the identified challenges and monitor progress.

As the school has determined areas of need and set specific, rigorous performance targets for improvement on key indicators through the data-based decision-making process, the leadership then initiates deliberations and discussions about improvement strategies. Key questions to consider in deciding about adopting strategies for change and improvement are:

- Is the school considering strategies targeted to specific goals and targets, as identified in the data-based decision-making process?
- What evidence exists to support the strategies under consideration? What is the quality of the evidence regarding each of the strategies?
- Is there widespread support for the adoption of the strategy? Is there confidence that the proposed strategy will lead to improved performance on the identified targets and goals?
- Are there the necessary conditions in the school (such as resources, knowledge, time) to implement the strategy? Is there professional development for the intervention strategy? (Levesque, Bradby, Rossi, & Teitelbaum, 1998)

The data-based decision-making process has most likely unearthed a number of areas for improvement and attention. Math achievement is declining in fourth and fifth grades, parent involvement is at an all-time low, and professional development has not been a top priority at the school. On what improvement efforts should Rosemont focus? How should these decisions be made?

Educational leaders can prioritize areas of need by addressing three key questions:

- How severe is the problem?
- How crucial or pressing is it to address this particular problem?
- How feasible is it for the school (given its resources, personnel, culture, context) to address the problem?

School leaders can involve the broader school community in deliberating about prioritizing needs. It makes the most sense to focus efforts on issues uncovered in the data-based decision-making processes, as described in the previous chapters, that are severe and crucial, but that are also under the control of the school, that is, it is something that the school can address. Clearly, improvement efforts should be focused on those areas that will have the strongest impact on student learning. If the staff prioritizes a problem emerging from the data as not feasible and not very severe, it would not make sense to expend too much effort on that issue.

In addition, intervention strategies should be targeted to outcomes for student learning and performance. Parent involvement and professional development are key pathways for student learning, and these pathways should be addressed in conjunction with interventions for addressing learning targets. If math achievement is the learning target, then professional development should be part of the intervention strategy for addressing mathematics achievement.

EVIDENCED-BASTED STRATEGIES

When deciding upon possible interventions and strategies to address a performance target or goal, educational leaders need to look at the educational research. As are other areas of education, educational research in the United States is also being shaped by No Child Left Behind. NCLB requires federal grantees to use their funds on *evidence-based strategies*, or *high-quality scientific research*.

The rationale seems to go something like this: The federal government spends money on education and basically says if schools want to receive federal money to implement programs and curricula, they have to indicate that the programs and practices schools implement are grounded in scientifically based research.

The U.S. federal government became involved in debates regarding education research because it had a relatively high level of discomfort about both the quality and impact of the research on education. In 2002, Dr. Grover J. Whitehurst, the director of the U.S. Department of Education's Institute of Educational Sciences (IES), the research arm of the federal education department, made the following statement:

> The National Research Council has concluded that the world of education, unlike defense, health care, or industrial production, does not rest on a strong research base. In no other field are

personal experience and ideology so frequently relied on to make policy choices, and in no other field is the research base so inadequate and little used. At the same time, the National Research Council has concluded that scientific inquiry in education is at its core the same as in all other fields. In other words, the core principles of scientific inquiry are as relevant for education as they are for medicine. There is every reason to believe that, if we invest in the education sciences and develop mechanisms to encourage evidence-based practice, we will see progress and transformation in education of the same order of magnitude as we have seen in medicine and agriculture. (Whitehurst, 2002)

It is fair to say that it was not only the federal government that had harsh words for the state of educational research. Education scholars themselves have lamented for decades about the quality of education research (Lagermann, 1997).

The Education Sciences Reform Act of 2002 (H.R. 3801; http://www.ed.gov/policy/rschstat/leg/PL107-279.pdf) established IES to support the type of high-quality research that can improve education. The goal of IES is "the transformation of education into an evidence-based field in which decision makers routinely seek out the best available research and data before adopting programs or practices that will affect significant numbers of students" and to "conduct and support scientifically valid research activities" (Education Sciences Reform Act p. 6, 2002).

Clearly, the interest in educational research from the perspective of informing policies, making programmatic decisions, and improving educational practices is a focus on research that "aims to support causal inferences about the efficacy of specific educational programs or policies" (Jacobs & Ludwig, 2005, p. 47). The discussion of scientifically based, evidence-based research is primarily about applied education research.

Therefore, educators, states, and leaders who depend on federal funding are now required to be aware of the nature of the research that guides their programs, decisions, and practices. In addition, educational researchers who wish to receive federal research monies also need to adhere to research designs that are compatible with accepted notions of scientifically based research.

We can think about these changes in terms of both supply and demand. "The supply of high-quality research is likely to be greatest in markets in which there is significant demand for the end product itself, and good research can be distinguished from bad" (Jacobs & Ludwig, 2005, p. 48). Focus on the quality of education research addresses supply-side issues, whereas changes in the incentives to adopt educational programs and decisions based on good research address the demand side. These perspectives obviously require an answer to the question, what is scientifically based research?

Under the No Child Left Behind Act, the term *scientifically based research* means research that "involves the application of rigorous, systematic, and objective procedures to obtain reliable and valid knowledge relevant to education activities and programs." (No Child Left Behind Act of 2001, p. 540). More broadly defined, it includes research that

- Employs systematic, empirical methods that draw on observation or experiment;
- Involves rigorous data analyses that are adequate to test the stated hypotheses and justify the general conclusions drawn;
- Relies on measurements or observational methods that provide reliable and valid data across evaluators and observers, across multiple measurements and observations and across studies by the same or different investigators;
- Is evaluated using experimental or quasi-experimental designs in which individuals, entities, programs or activities are assigned to different conditions and with appropriate controls to evaluate the effects of the condition of interest, with a preference for random-assignment experiments, or other designs to the extent that those designs contain within-condition or across-condition controls;
- Ensures experimental studies are presented in sufficient detail and clarity to allow for replication or, at a minimum, offer the opportunity to build systematically on their findings; and
- Has been accepted by a peer-reviewed journal or approved by a panel of independent experts through a comparably rigorous, objective and scientific review. (Public law 107–11, Section III).

As can be imagined, there was great trepidation among scholars and researchers with this renewed government involvement in education research. In the past research was more of a "bottom up" type of enterprise; that is, researchers in the field would initiate research ideas.

Educational researchers worried that the good intentions underlying the SBR (scientifically based research) movement would go astray, narrowing definitions of research or science that might trivialize rather than enrich our understanding of education policy and practice and that the benefits of unfettered scholarship would be eroded by conformity and methodological zealotry. Almost everyone can appreciate intuitively the advantages of evidence-based policy; it is another matter entirely to make this concept clear, operational, and valid (Feuer, Towne, & Shavelson, 2002, p. 4).

The federal legislation was a call for researchers to look at themselves and clean house. "Why do lawmakers feel compelled to codify methods of educational research in federal statute? Perhaps it is because they do not trust the field to monitor itself. The tension in the case of educational research reflects a crisis of confidence during a particularly important time in its history that must be addressed if the field is to take full advantage of the present opportunity" (Feuer et al., 2002, p. 8).

Lee Shulman, the president of the Carnegie Foundation for the Advancement of Teaching, wrote a commentary published in *Education Week* about the new thrust on evidence-based policymaking. His essay is called "Seek Simplicity . . . and Distrust It." He maintains that even with "good" evidence, we know that research often reaches different and conflicting conclusions. Shulman said, "Research is all about exercising judgment under conditions of uncertainty, and even experimental designs don't relieve us of those judgmental burdens. The acts of designing experiments themselves invoke value judgments, and interpreting the results always demands judgment." This does not mean that research is unnecessary or that education decisions cannot be based on careful research. "We need to recognize that research evidence rarely speaks directly to the resolution of policy controversy without the necessary mediating agencies of human judgment, human values, and community of scholars and actors prepared to deliberate and weigh alternatives in the world of uncertainty" (Shulman, 2005, p. 36).

The implications of this shift for educators and school leaders are profound. On some topics research is emerging that addresses questions about what works and under what conditions specific strategies or interventions may work. This research can serve as an important knowledge base for determining how to address problems identified by the data-based decision-making processes.

What Types of Research Can Best Inform Decision Making?

The term *research* is used widely. Most important for data-based decision making is research regarding the effect or outcome of school-based interventions or strategies. Certain types of research can best answer the question, what works? Research that addresses whether an intervention works, that caused the intended effects, is referred to as *experimental design*. Perhaps one of the most fundamental distinctions in understanding the quality of research that can inform decision making is the difference between experimental designs and nonexperimental designs.

The best evidence used to instruct it is dictated by law (NCLB)

Experimental Designs

What is an experimental design? An experimental design is a research design where a *treatment*, or in our case an intervention or strategy, is given to subjects or participants to measure whether the intervention causes a change in behavior.

A simple example of an experiment would be the following: A researcher takes all the fifth graders in a district and randomly assigns half of the students to the curriculum currently in use and the other half to a new curriculum based on a problem-centered approach that spirals the curriculum and makes connections across topics and other subject matters. The researcher uses measures of students' math achievement from the spring before the experiment begins (while the students were in fourth grade) and measures math achievement again at the end of each of three years (i.e., in fifth, sixth, and seventh grades). The students' change in math knowledge and skills is tested before the implementation of the new curriculum and at the end of each school year for three years, in both the treatment classes (the students receiving the new curriculum) and the control classes (those students still receiving the current curriculum). In a true experiment, participants (students in our example) are randomly assigned to the intervention, the new curriculum, or the control group, the existing curriculum. *Random assignment* means that each participant (students in our example) has an equal chance of being assigned to either group. This is important because it prevents bias. For example, it prevents all the students who are highly motivated in math from being assigned to the new curriculum or all the students with high achievement scores in math from being assigned to the current curriculum group, the control group.

Sometimes it is not possible to randomly assign participants—students, for example—into groups. Researchers often then rely on intact groups such as students who are already assigned to their classroom teachers. In this case half of the classrooms would receive the current curriculum and half the classrooms would receive the new curriculum. When it is not possible to randomly assign students, the research design is a called a *quasi-experimental design*. Much research in education is quasi-experimental because students are already assigned to classrooms and teachers and principals are already working in schools when a new program or method is being researched. When it is not possible to randomly assign participants in an experiment, researchers implementing quasi-experimental designs attempt to match the participants in the two groups on important characteristics such as demographic characteristics and prior achievement levels.

However, it is important to note that the conclusions drawn from quasi-experimental designs regarding the impact or effect of a program, intervention, or new approach are usually not as strong as those of a true experiment are. The reason that conclusions from studies that do not implement random assignment must be interpreted with caution is that the two groups, the group receiving the intervention and the comparison group, the students receiving the traditional curriculum, for example, may not be equivalent. Random assignment ensures that the two groups were initially the same at the beginning of the experiment.

When random assignment is not used, the two groups could differ in many ways: motivation, ability, the extent to which students complete math homework each night, the parents' support at home, and so on. Therefore, if the students in the new curriculum outperform students in the current curriculum, it would be hard to know if this was caused by the new curriculum or if the differences could be attributed to differences in the two groups of students, such all the high-ability students being placed in the new problem-centered curriculum classes.

It is important to note that some research relies on very weak designs such as using just one group of students and giving them some type of test before an intervention and another test at the end of the intervention. Imagine a classroom teacher giving her students a math test and then adding a new problem-solving method to her teaching and giving her students a test again at the end of the semester and telling all the teachers across the state that her students' grades increased and they should follow her teaching methods exactly. Could she attribute the change in grades to the new problem-solving method? *NO.* Without a comparison group, there is no way to tell if the students would have performed equally well or better with other methods. In addition, perhaps the students performed better simply because they matured during the course of the year. Or maybe this teacher had all the gifted students in her class. There are many other alternative explanations that can explain the results.

In summary, when evaluating experimental designs it is important to scrutinize the research for three key aspects: random assignment, a comparison group, and pre- and postmeasures of change. The checklist shown in Figure 9.1, developed by the U.S. Department of Education, provides a framework that can be used to decide if research meets the standards of rigor that should be used for making decisions regarding adopting an educational intervention or strategy.

In addition to the quality of the research design, a number of other aspects of the research should be considered, as noted by The Center for Data-Driven Reform in Education at Johns Hopkins University (www .cddre.org). The duration of a study is very important. The optimal time to determine if an intervention has an effect is at least one school year. Research based on the results of less than a year should be interpreted with caution. Of course, longitudinal studies that study the results of the intervention over time can provide even more valid results. We know that change takes time.

Next, it is important to know if the results of the study have been replicated, that is, similar results have been reported in other studies. For example, are there three or more studies that have found a positive effect of peer tutoring on achievement in mathematics or just one study? If there are a number of studies pointing to the same results, we would have more confidence that implementation in our school would also yield positive results.

We would place more confidence in studies conducted by outside (third-party) researchers rather than by the researchers who developed the intervention. There is less likely to be bias if the evaluators and researchers are independent from the program designers and implementers. Furthermore, research that is published in peer-reviewed journals, journals that scrutinize the quality of the research design and methods as well as the validity of the results and conclusions, should be considered stronger than research that is on a Web page or in a report that has not undergone a rigorous, independent review.

Figure 9.1 How to Evaluate Whether an Educational Intervention Is Supported by Rigorous Evidence: An Overview

Step 1. Is the intervention backed by "strong" evidence of effectiveness?

Quality of studies needed to establish "strong" evidence:
- Randomized controlled trials that are well designed and well implemented.

Quantity of evidence needed:
- Trials showing effectiveness in two or more typical school settings,
- Including a setting similar to that of your schools/classrooms.

Step 2. If the intervention is not backed by "strong" evidence, is it backed by "possible" evidence of effectiveness?

Types of studies that can comprise "possible" evidence:
- Randomized controlled trials whose quality/quantity are good but fall short of "strong" evidence; and/or
- Comparison-group studies in which the intervention and comparison groups are *very closely matched* in academic achievement, demographics, and other characteristics.

(Continued)

(Continued)

Types of studies that do not comprise "possible" evidence:

• Pre/post studies.

• Comparison-group studies in which the intervention and comparison groups are not closely matched.

• "Meta-analyses" that include the results of such lower-quality studies.

Step 3. If the answers to both questions above are "no," one may conclude that the intervention is not supported by meaningful evidence.

SOURCE: U.S. Department of Education (2003). *Identifying and Implementing Educational Practices Supported By Rigorous Evidence: A User Friendly Guide* http://ies.ed.gov/ncee/wwc/pdf/rigorousevid.pdf

The What Works Clearinghouse was established in 2002 by IES to provide educators, policymakers, researchers, and the public with a source of scientific evidence of what works in education (www.whatworks.ed.gov). The What Works Clearinghouse develops reports based on a review of available research regarding the effectiveness of educational interventions on improving student outcomes. The clearinghouse also rates the quality of evidence available to determine the effectiveness of an intervention strategy. Following are two examples of reviews from What Works Clearinghouse of two elementary school math curricula, Everyday Math and Saxton Math. Based on the reviews of evidence available to date, Everyday Math has more empirical research evidence available to suggest that it can lead to positive outcomes for children in mathematics.

Nonexperimental designs. Nonexperimental research studies do not involve an intervention or treatment implemented by the researcher. It is often impractical, too difficult, or too costly to implement an experiment. Often, then, researchers observe, measure, or describe a phenomenon or condition and then try to look at the past to try to identify possible causes of the condition. The researchers are not implementing the intervention because it has already occurred. This type of study is called a *causal-comparative* or *ex-post facto* study. For example, a researcher may try to explain why some math teachers have students who all have passed a proficiency test over the past three years, whereas another set of teachers' students do not pass. The researcher then sets out to examine and explain the factors that could account for the differences between the two groups of students and their teachers, such as how much time the teachers spent on math instruction, which curriculum they implemented, how much homework and what types of homework were assigned, and so on.

Figure 9.2 Everyday Mathematics

Program Description	*Everyday Mathematics*, published by Wright Group/McGraw-Hill, is a core curriculum for students in kindergarten through Grade 6 covering numeration and order, operations, functions and sequences, data and chance, algebra, geometry and spatial sense, measures and measurement, reference framers, and patterns. At each grade level, the *Everyday Mathematics* curriculum provides students with multiple opportunities to learn concepts and practice skills. Across grade levels, concepts are reviewed and extended in varying instructional contexts. The distinguishing features of *Everyday Mathematics* are its focus on real-life problem solving, student communication of mathematical thinking, and appropriate use of technology. This curriculum also emphasizes balancing different types of instruction, using various methods for skills practice, and fostering parent involvement in student learning.
Research	Four studies of *Everyday Mathematics* met the What Works Clearinghouse (WWC) evidence standards with reservations. These studies included a total of approximately 12,600 students in Grades 3–5 from a range of socioeconomic backgrounds and attending schools in urban, suburban, and rural communities in multiple states. The WWC considers the content of evidence for *Everyday Mathematics* to be moderate to large for math achievement.
Effectiveness	*Everyday Mathematics* was found to have potentially positive effects on students' math achievement.

Math Achievement	
Rating of effectiveness	Potentially positive effects
Improvement index	Average: +6 percentile points Range: −7 to +14 percentile points

SOURCE: What Works Clearinghouse (2007c) http://ies.ed.gov/ncee/wwc/reports/elementary_math/eday_math/

In this type of research design, if the researcher finds that the students who meet proficiency tend to have teachers who teach in a very student-centered approach, whereas students who do not meet proficiency tend to have teachers who are more skill-based, one cannot conclude that teacher focus and style cause the differences in student achievement. The only conclusion warranted is that teacher style and focus are associated with or related to student proficiency. Thus the conclusions of nonexperimental designs are not as strong as those of experimental designs in terms of understanding causation.

Figure 9.3 Saxon Elementary School Math

Program description	*Saxon Elementary School Math*, published by Harcourt Achieve, is a core curriculum for students in kindergarten through Grade 5. A distinguishing feature of *Saxon Elementary School Math* is its use of a distributed approach, as opposed to a chapter-based approach, for instruction and assessment. The program is built on the premise that students learn best when instruction is incremental and explicit, previously learned concepts are continually reviewed, and assessment is frequent and cumulative. At each grade level, math concepts are introduced, reviewed, and practiced over time in order to move students from understanding to mastery to fluency. For Grades K–3, the *Saxon Elementary School Math* curriculum emphasizes hands-on activities and teacher-directed math conversations that engage students in learning. The curriculum for Grades 4–5 also uses math conversations to introduce new concepts, but shifts the focus to student-directed learning.
Research	One study of the *Saxon Elementary School Math* program met the What Works Clearinghouse (WWC) evidence standards with reservations. The study included students in Grades 1–8 from a range of socioeconomic backgrounds and attending 342 schools across the state of Georgia. This report focuses only on findings for Grades 1–5. The WWC considers the extent of evidence for *Saxon Elementary School Math* to be small for math achievement.
Effectiveness	*Saxon Elementary School Math* was found to have no discernible effects on math achievement.

	Math Achievement	
	Rating of effectiveness	No descriptive effects
	Improvement index	Not Applicable

SOURCE: What Works Clearinghouse (2007b) http://ies.ed.gov/ncee/wwc/reports/elementary_math/sesm/index.asp

Other types of nonexperimental studies include surveys used to describe attitudes, beliefs, and behaviors, as noted in earlier chapters. We can survey teachers over a number of years, called a *longitudinal survey*, to gauge the extent to which they are implementing the activities and practices called for in a new curriculum. Correlation research designs examine whether there is a relationship or association between two or more domains. Through correlational studies researchers have examined whether there is a relationship between years of teaching experience and types of teacher training and student achievement. It is very important to note that a correlation or an association between two factors does not mean that one factor caused the other one.

The important point is that only through experimental designs can educators begin to address questions of causality. Does the intervention, the new program, the change in strategy cause the desired outcome? The other types of studies can provide information about the question under study but cannot provide the rigorous evidence needed to claim cause and effect. These research designs can be used to inform your decisions but cannot answer the question about what works with the same level of certainty as experimental designs.

In summary, as the leadership team begins to deliberate about possible interventions and strategies to adopt to address specific goals, examining current educational research will help the team know if the intervention has been researched and whether it has led to positive outcomes for children. Not all research is the same; thus the conclusions the team reaches should be based on the careful review of the quality of the research evidence. The What Works Clearinghouse and other research reviews are important resources.

Beyond learning from the results of research, research can also help the leadership team understand what is involved in implementing a particular strategy or program. Most research includes a detailed report of the nature of the program being implemented.

When deciding to implement an intervention based on rigorous research evidence, you need to pay close attention to the details of the implementation of the strategy or intervention in *YOUR* school. Often a strategy does not lead to the desired results in a new setting because it was not implemented properly, and the details of the implementation were not followed carefully. This is called *implementation fidelity*. Furthermore, it is extremely important to provide the necessary training, professional development, and supports for high-quality implementation.

PROMISING PRACTICES: LEARNING FROM OTHERS

In addition to examining rigorous research evidence, many educators consider other promising practices that they learn about from their professional networks and expert practitioners in their schools and districts. What should leadership look for when exploring promising strategies that may not have a sufficient research base?

It is important to articulate specifically what the purpose, goal, and outcomes of the practice are. Not all fads should be considered promising practices. What makes this practice promising? What is the evidence? From whom is the evidence provided? How widespread is the evidence about the effect of the practice under consideration, in the absence of high-quality scientific research?

There is a set of other considerations when reviewing promising practices:

- Is the setting and context similar to the one you are considering? For example, if you work in a large middle school in a rural district and the promising practice has been implemented in a small private elementary school, what can you learn?
- Are the participants similar? For example, the promising practice may involve veteran teachers who were reluctant to learn new teaching pedagogies, whereas your teachers are a very diverse group with many first-year teachers. It is important to take into account other participants when learning about promising practices and how they are similar to and different from your students, teachers, community, and so on.
- Is the intervention aligned with other programs currently in place?
- Is there clarity regarding the implementation? What was the strategy? How was it implemented? What is the timing of implementing the various aspects of the intervention? Can the implementation strategies be replicated in your school? Are there materials to serve as a guide?
- What is the level of support and expertise needed to implement the practice? Were there specific financial supports such as grants or new personnel? Was there expertise that you may or may not have at your school? In other words, what does it take to implement this promising program or practice?
- What were the specific results, impact, and outcomes of this practice? Why is it considered promising? By whom?
- What are possible barriers to implementation and success?

The Center for Data-Driven Reform (www.cddre.org) has suggested guidelines for using research in making decisions about intervention strategies that can also be used when reviewing both research and promising practices from other educators. The center suggests carefully reviewing the intervention to determine that it is a good fit and relevant to the goals being targeted. An intervention targeted toward improving discipline in the school would not be aligned with the target goal of mathematics instruction if the data-based decision-making process determined that the school culture and climate, including student behavior, was very strong and not a challenge that needed to be addressed. Your school should also consider the extent to which the new intervention strategy is aligned or consistent with programs already in place. If your school is organized in traditional grade structures and students stay in their classes for all of their instruction, with no grouping by ability outside of the classroom, adopting an intervention strategy that requires regrouping may not fit with the current programs or the school's culture.

As noted earlier it is very important to know in advance whether there are professional development and coaching for the successful implementation of the intervention. Depending on the specifics of the intervention, professional development and coaching do not necessarily have to come from outside the school. Sometimes there is expertise from existing faculty and school leaders or from the district. Often, however, professional development and coaching need to be part of the implementation strategy with expertise and support from those who have been involved in successful implementation.

When considering an intervention, you also need to note the extent to which the intervention is specified and described in enough detail so that others can fully understand and replicate it. Is there sufficient detail so teachers can implement the program? And, lastly, it is important to determine what interim measures of accountability are available in your school for ongoing monitoring and feedback. Does the program include opportunities for frequent observation and discussion to provide feedback? We turn to this point about ongoing monitoring toward the end of this chapter.

Decision Models for Setting a Path of Implementation and Improvement

Once your leadership team has gathered and reviewed information from research and promising practices, as well as putting forth its own ideas for addressing the targeted goals, your school must make decisions about what avenues to pursue. Typically, there is more than one possible solution to address a given issue identified through the data. The information-gathering stage most likely has unearthed a number of possible strategies. Making a decision about which strategies to implement is a very important step in data-based decision making.

Adopting a strategy, practice, or intervention should first be decided with the goal of choosing the best option to propel your school from where it currently stands (as diagnosed by the data) to where it hopes to be in terms of attaining its new goals. Thus if your school diagnosed math as one of the core problems facing the school in a number of areas—student achievement, professional development, and parent involvement—the strategies adopted will focus on addressing math instruction.

Hoy and Tarter (2004) have developed a simplified decision-making model that can be applied as a team begins to determine what path or strategy to take to meet the school's goals. One question a school leader needs to address when deciding which strategy to implement is, who should be involved in the decision? The concept of a *zone of acceptance* can be helpful here. If school faculty members feel that the decision is relevant to their work (i.e., they have a personal stake in the decision), and they have expertise to contribute, then the decision falls outside the zone of acceptance, and they should be involved. Teachers who teach math have a personal stake in changes in math instruction and curriculum, and they have expertise; thus they should be involved in the decisions regarding choosing strategies. On the other hand, if teachers have no stake (i.e., there is no personal relevance and no expertise to contribute to the decision making), then the decision is within a zone of acceptance, and the teachers can be excluded. Reading teachers may not have as much of a stake or have much expertise to contribute to the decision regarding adopting a new math instructional program.

Involving teachers in the decision about which strategy to adopt is important; broad support can enhance the likelihood of success. However, not all interventions are the same, and some have a stronger evidence base than others. In addition, the strategy should be specifically targeted to a performance goal (e.g., increasing parent involvement in support of mathematics, changing the professional development opportunities for teachers to implement a new mathematics curriculum) so that its impact can be evaluated and monitored in light of ongoing data-based decision-making and school-improvement processes. Lastly, it is important to consider the likelihood of success in the particular context. Leaders know their schools, their communities, and their settings. Not every intervention is aligned with the local culture and context of a school, its community, and its existing programs and policies.

Figure 9.3 Rosemont Leadership Team Chooses an Intervention

The principal at Rosemont School assembled the grade-level coordinators for an initial meeting to begin the process of choosing an intervention to address the new goals in mathematics in light of the new performance targets. After the initial meeting, a group of teachers with expertise in mathematics was recruited to participate in the leadership team that would select the new strategy, following the guidelines of a simplified decision-making model.

At the initial meeting of the strategy selection team, the principal set forth the process the group would use to choose a strategy, including looking at scientific evidence. The principal handed out two studies that proposed two instructional strategies, and the group practiced using criteria for evaluating research against one of the studies. The principal explained the criteria and helped the group understand them. The group then divided up into two teams, and each team was charged with reporting back in two weeks a review of other research and discussions with the district mathematics coordinator and other contacts identified from neighboring districts and professional associations. All intervention strategies will be evaluated against the same criteria—including mission central—to determine which strategy is most likely to impact the performance target of mathematics achievement.

CONTINUOUS PERFORMANCE MONITORING

This section describes the steps needed to monitor and evaluate the strategies adopted. Your school examined its goals and mission, analyzed data to define specific areas of focus and need, and examined the research and promising practices to decide upon specific interventions and strategies for improvement. Deciding to adopt an intervention or strategy is a commitment to action. An implementation plan is key. Improvement efforts cannot succeed without a clear plan for implementation. The objective of the implementation plan is to continue to collect important data on an ongoing basis, interpret trends in implementation and performance, and modify or sustain the plan of action. Charting growth and change is a central goal of continuous improvement.

From a data-based decision-making perspective, there are three key steps in continuous monitoring of the implementation of strategies for improvement:

1. Define criteria for interim monitoring and evaluation.

2. Set priorities for ongoing data collection.

3. Determine frequency of data collection and reporting.

Defining Criteria for Interim Monitoring and Evaluation

Interim data monitoring should focus on two factors: implementation and impact. In terms of the implementation, it is important to monitor whether the intervention strategy is being implemented as planned. If there is a clear plan for implementation, monitoring becomes relatively easy. As the school adapts a new mathematics instructional strategy, the plan may include the following steps, as noted in the planning guide, Table 9.1.

1. Present to the faculty the data that lead to the identification of math achievement as the focus of a new improvement strategy in the school.

2. Review the processes undertaken to decide upon an intervention strategy (the research review, the analysis of alternatives).

3. Establish grade-level planning teams, professional development, ongoing curriculum development work, peer observations, review of lesson plans, student work and so on.

Each step can be monitored for implementation.

Table 9.1 Planning and Monitoring Guide for Implementation

Goal	Strategy	Action Steps
Improve student achievement in mathematics	Implement problem-centered mathematics instruction	1.1 Presentation and background to all faculty 1.2 Grade-level planning teams 1.3 Professional development 1.4 First wave of implementation 1.5 Teacher study groups
Responsibility	Timeline	Monitoring
Who's going to accomplish the action?	When will action be started and accomplished?	1.1 Date 1.2 Reporting back about the meetings 1.3 When attend, how many attend

In addition to monitoring implementation, it is crucial to monitor ongoing progress toward reaching the goal of improved mathematics achievement. It would be imprudent to wait for a year after implementation and rely merely on measures of standardized achievement tests to assess change. In deciding upon interim monitoring, leaders and teachers should take into account the *proximate goals* of changes in the instructional strategies in mathematics as well as the *ultimate goals*. An ultimate goal is the final outcome goal, in this case changes in mathematics achievement. However, there are proximate goals, or changes that are very close to the implementation of the instructional strategy, such as assignments focused on problem solving, more learner-centered instruction, more students achieving higher on the district's formative assessments, teacher collaboration across grade levels, fewer failing grades on report cards each six weeks, and so on. These could be indicators that change is moving in the right direction. Each of these proximate goals can serve as the basis for interim monitoring of the intervention.

Setting Priorities for Ongoing Monitoring

Of course, continuous improvement monitoring should not be so cumbersome that the entire faculty's energy is being usurped by monitoring rather than implementing and teaching. Therefore, it is important to focus on indicator data that are most important for understanding progress toward achieving the ultimate goal, improving students' mathematics achievement and learning. In our case of mathematics, it would be important to monitor the ongoing formative assessments in use by the district. Putting into place a system of peer observations by teachers teaching the same grade level could provide valuable ongoing feedback about implementing the changes in mathematics instruction. Devoting teacher planning time to sharing student work can be another type of data that helps monitor ongoing implementation. School leaders will put into place a plan to share the data from ongoing monitoring at regular team meetings.

Determining Frequency of Data Collection and Reporting

A plan for presenting and discussing the progress and implementation of the change process helps teachers modify their practices as your school examines the data. Data that sit on a shelf in a binder are not useful; data are useful when your school community interprets and discusses them. Set out a plan noting when each of the data types will be presented for analysis and discussion. Key questions for discussion include the following: What do we learn from the data? How can we change our practices? Are we moving toward our performance target and goals? Ongoing monitoring can be distributed among the teachers involved in the particular change; thus mathematics teachers can rotate presenting the data and leading the discussion about lessons learned and next steps. Through a planned process of implementation and monitoring, the school can clearly assess progress toward meeting its goals through the data-based decision-making process.

CONCLUSION

The process of data-based decision making helps determine areas of focus and need in your school. It can only go so far in helping determine the best strategy and intervention to begin to bring about change and improvement.

After prioritizing areas of need in the school, a simplified decision-making model can bring together a motivated and interested team of teachers and leaders to work together to choose an intervention and set out a path for implementation and ongoing monitoring and feedback.

In this chapter we described a process for choosing an intervention strategy based on high-quality scientific evidence and best practices. We noted that it is important to understand the criteria for scientific evidence as well as take into account the local context when making a decision about choosing a strategy for improvement. Experimental designs provide the best research evidence to determine what works and under what conditions.

Once a strategy is implemented, ongoing monitoring with data aligned with the proximate goals of the program can help modify implementation and provide important feedback regarding how the new strategies are working and whether the intended impact is likely to be realized. Midcourse corrections can be made based on the ongoing monitoring and feedback.

Taken together, a strategy that involves specifying clear goals for improvement based on data and a review of high-quality research in conjunction with the expertise of educators, coupled with a visible planned process of monitoring and feedback, is likely to bring about real change.

Discussion Questions

1. Why is scientifically based evidence so important, and how can it be used by the leadership team to explore intervention strategies?

2. What key issues should a leadership team address when reviewing research?

3. Visit the What Works Clearinghouse (www.whatworks.ed.gov) and review the quality of the evidence for interventions in reading.

4. What data are available for ongoing monitoring of the proximate goals of a writing instructional program?

Leading With Data for Continuous School Improvement

10

Based on identifying the problem and selecting solutions to address this problem, this chapter revisits leading with data for continuous improvement. Using the rich array of data to measure the pathways to address the mission of your school, the discovery process for finding your school's strengths and weaknesses continues. Data-based decision making is ongoing. New problems may emerge that require different interventions. You can lead your school community to engage in these issues time and time again.

VIGNETTE REVISITED

Your school has measured its mission, identified problem areas, and examined scientifically based interventions. Your teams have done their homework to examine the evidence supporting different interventions that address the school's challenges. Rosemont teachers and you have determined the criteria for monitoring and evaluating the interventions and have set priorities and timelines for data collection. The district superintendent is impressed with your, comprehensive and evidence-based plan. So, too, your parents have engaged in your efforts. Problem found, addressed, and solved. You're done, right? No. Leading with data is continuous. It's an ongoing cycle. Time—and data—will tell whether the current problems have been transformed into school strengths. Perhaps the current challenges continue. Perhaps new ones

---

> emerge. Using the approaches provided in previous chapters, you can lead your school with a rich array of data linked to mission and embedded into continuous school-improvement processes that involve your school's community.

We began by asking the question, why is using data for decision making important for school improvement? We argued and, we hope, convinced you that effective educational leaders use data extensively to guide decision making, to set and prioritize goals, and to monitor progress. Continuous analysis of the divide between student learning goals and actual performance defines the actions of effective schools. Relying on a broad array of data, not just test scores, educational leaders can identify challenges, implement interventions, and monitor and evaluate progress.

The school's mission is the starting point. It plays a crucial role in guiding all the programs and activities within the school. Measuring the mission provides the opportunity for school leaders to examine data, whether that is achievement scores or other indicators of pathways for effective schools. Thus school leaders must continually engage data to set strategic goals consistent with the vision and mission of their school and address key school effectiveness indicators.

Throughout the preceding chapters, we laid out the details of using data to strengthen schools. Figure 10.1 portrays this process, which we discussed in Chapter 3. We first evaluated how you can assess your school's mission statement. We discussed the pathways and ways to measure them to link data to the mission. Next, we talked about compiling the data for benchmarking the outcomes and processes, which may involve standardized achievement scores, formative assessments, and other data used for measuring the pathways to improve your school. We then discussed how to involve the school community to analyze the data to identify a problem in your school. We provided examples about how to analyze all the data across several school years, peeling the onion in a variety of ways to dig deep into the data to understand your school's strengths and weaknesses. By identifying the key problems, we were able to point the direction toward using scientifically based interventions to address the problems in your school.

Even though improving schools with data involves more than just test scores, standardized achievement scores are important, particularly those on the state assessments. These achievement scores provide a key source of data to understand how well students are learning—at the school, classroom, and individual levels. Although not the only source, schools, principals, and teachers are accountable for student learning based on these standardized assessments within the current policy environment. After our discussion of the variety of test scores and the way they are reported, we hope that you have a more thorough understanding about how they can provide a way for your school to understand what it does well and what areas need additional work.

Figure 10.1 Continuous Steps in the Process of Using Data to Strengthen Schools

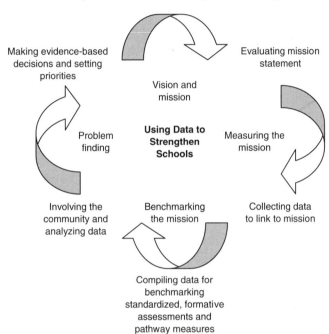

Making evidence-based decisions and setting priorities

Evaluating mission statement

Vision and mission

Using Data to Strengthen Schools

Problem finding

Measuring the mission

Involving the community and analyzing data

Benchmarking the mission

Collecting data to link to mission

Compiling data for benchmarking standardized, formative assessments and pathway measures

Although important, state assessments are not the only source of data for measuring how well the students in your school are performing. Other types of assessments exist to understand how well students are doing throughout the year. These formative, or benchmark, assessments provide additional resources to teachers. Formative assessment systems provide teachers with ongoing information regarding their students, with specific information about different subdomains of subject areas. This specific, timely information can help teachers diagnose specific areas of need and thus modify instruction. Formative assessments are also used to provide the basis for powerful professional development linked to specific student-learning goals.

Other pathways to school improvement are critical, and we discussed not only what these pathways are but also how they can be measured. We discussed how additional data can inform processes toward improvement goals. As we showed in Chapter 2, school mission and goals are at the center, with the other indicators supporting that mission and the entire school improvement set of processes supported by a foundation of continuous data-based decision making. Although schools face an overabundance of data, these indicators are the building blocks of a school's capacity for continuous improvement. The specific school-improvement indicators we discussed included shared mission and goals; rigorous content standards for all students—agreed upon, understood, and measurable; alignment to standards—curriculum and instructional coherence; expert teachers supported by coherent, consistent professional development; professional community; partnerships with parents, families, and community; culture and climate for student learning; resources aligned to goals; and data-based processes for analyzing programs, practices, and results.

We stressed that leaders can look at pathways for effective schools as a bundle of schooling activities and processes, overlapping and mutually supportive. At the foundation, however, is the use of data-based processes for analyzing programs, practices, and results regarding each indicator to support student performance, learning, and achievement—the critical aims of schooling.

Involving the parents and school community is crucial in the data-based school-improvement process. We discussed several effective strategies for connecting schools, families, and communities to promote student learning. We described the benefits associated with involving communities in schools, presented ways to develop collaborative community and family engagement in data-based decision making and collecting data about the school community.

After describing the importance of data-based decisions and the array of different achievement scores and pathways to effective schools, we provided an example of where school leaders get started in looking at their school's data. The school mission was the starting point, as we described the overall achievement levels of the school and started to peel the onion. We peeled and peeled. We disaggregated the data in a variety of ways to identify potential problems to address with various school-improvement strategies. We arrived at some specific issues on which Rosemont should focus its efforts. Based on this illustration, we hope that you are better prepared to think about your school's data and how to analyze these data in a number of ways to help your school community focus on specific school challenges.

We also provided information about how to set priorities for school improvement and identify possible strategies to address school weaknesses. We presented a variety of resources to identify research-based programs and approaches to address issues related to curriculum, instruction, professional development, and other school-improvement interventions. We also discussed the importance of scientifically based research and how to think about whether school interventions have a strong research base. Our hope is that you and your school have a better understanding about how to examine your school's problems and to think about research-based interventions and how they may fit your current school context.

In addition, we emphasized that data-based decision making for school improvement is a never-ending process. We encouraged you to think about, gather data, and assess whether the interventions you implement are actually having the effects your school anticipated. Only through this continuous monitoring can you and your school know that you are continuously improving. Some problems may be solved. Some new ones may arise. Gathering a variety of data indicators, analyzing them, and building your school community are critical for school leaders to lead with data.

What happened to Rosemont? We do not have a definitive answer for that question. However, as we described, the leadership team at Rosemont School worked hard to help teachers and the community understand the importance of data-based decision making. They made great progress in using data to focus priorities. Compiling and then analyzing data, team members identified specific pathways and challenges to address. They found specific problems and prioritized their needs such as focusing on math achievement in Grades 4 and 5, distributing their highly qualified teachers, and involving their parents in academic activities. To address these challenges, the team was able to assess the scientifically based interventions to address the problems of their school. The team also put in place a process to monitor the progress of implementation and whether the school was meeting its needs.

Rosemont engaged in a process of data-based decision making in a systematic, thoughtful manner. As with any endeavor with school improvement, there were likely some high points and some low points as administrators and teachers implemented their school-improvement strategies. Throughout, the school was able to engage in the data-based decision-making processes to move forward with evidence about their activities to address their challenges. Such thought, effort, and continuous engagement is our hope for all schools—and those that lead them, teach in them, and learn in them—to build on strengths, address weaknesses, and seize opportunities for success.

References

Adams, J. E., & Kirst, M. W. (1999). New demands and concepts for educational accountability: Striving for results in an era of accountability. In J. Murphy & K. Louis (Eds.), *Handbook of research on educational administration* (2nd ed.). (pp. 463–489). San Francisco: Jossey-Bass.

Adler, P. S. (1991, June). *NUMMI, Circa 1988* (Management report). Palo Alto, CA: Stanford University, Department of Industrial Engineering and Engineering.

American Educational Research Association. (2004). Teachers matter: Evidence from value-added assessments. *Research Points, 2*(20), 1–4.

Ariaza, G. (2004). *Making changes that stay made: School reform and community involvement.* Chapel Hill: The University of North Carolina Press.

Baker, E. L. (2002). Teacher use of formal assessment in the classroom. In W. D. Hawley (Ed.), *The keys to effective schools: Educational reform as continuous improvement* (pp. 56–64). Thousand Oaks, CA: Corwin Press.

Bamburg, J., & Andrews, R. (1990). School goals, principals, and achievement. *School Effectiveness and School Improvement, 2,* 175–191.

Barr, R., & Dreeben, R. (1983). *How schools work.* Chicago: University of Chicago Press.

Belfield, C. R., & Levin, H. (2005). *Privatization of school choice: Consequences for parents, schools, and public policy.* Boulder, CO: Paradigm Publishers.

Benson, T. (1993, July 5). Quality: If at first you don't succeed. *Industry Week,* 48–49.

Berends, M. (2004). In the wake of *A Nation At Risk*: New American Schools' private sector school reform initiative. *Peabody Journal of Education, 79*(1), 130–163.

Berends, M. (2006). Survey research methods in educational research. In J. Green, G. Camilli, & P. Elmore (Eds.), *Handbook of complementary methods for research in education* (pp. 521–538). Mahwah, NJ: Lawrence Erlbaum Associates.

Berends, M., Bodilly, S., & Kirby, S. N. (2002). *Facing the challenges of whole-school reform: New American schools after a decade.* Santa Monica, CA: RAND.

Berends, M., Kirby, S. N., Naftel, S., & McKelvey, C. (2001). *Implementation and performance in New American Schools: Three years into scale-up.* Santa Monica, CA: RAND.

Berends, M., Lucas, S. R., Sullivan, T., & Briggs, R.J. (2005). *Examining gaps in mathematics achievement among racial-ethnic groups, 1972–1992.* Santa Monica, CA: RAND.

Berends, M., & Zottola, G. (in press). A primer on survey methods. In S. Lapan & M. L. Quartaroli (Eds.), *Methods in educational research.* San Francisco: Jossey-Bass.

Berliner, D. C. & Biddle, B. J. (1995). *The manufactured crisis: Myths, fraud, and the attack on America's public schools.* New York: Addison-Wesley.

Betts, J. R., & Grogger, J. (2003). The impact of grading standards on student achievement, educational attainment, and entry-level earnings. *Economics of Education Review, 22,* 34–52.

Bidwell, C., & Friedkin, N. (1988). Sociology of education. In N. J. Smelser (Ed.), *Handbook of sociology* (pp. 449–471). Thousand Oaks, CA: Sage.

Black, P., & Wiliam, D. (1998a). Assessment and classroom learning. *Assessment in Education, 5,* 4.

Black, P., & Wiliam, D. (1998b). Inside the black box: Raising standards through classroom assessment. *Phi Delta Kappan, 80,* 139–149.

Bodilly, S., & Berends, M. (1999). Necessary district support for comprehensive school reform. In G. Orfield & E. H. DeBray (Eds.), *Hard work for good schools: Facts not fads in Title I reform* (pp. 111–119). Boston: Harvard University, Civil Rights Project.

Boston, C. (2002). The concept of formative assessment. *Practical Assessment, Research and Evaluation, 8*(9). Retrieved January 8, 2007, from http://PAREonline.net

Bransford, J., Brown, A., & Cocking, R. (Eds.). (1999). *How people learn: Brain, mind, experience and school.* Washington, DC: Commission on Behavioral and Social Sciences and Education, National Research Council. National Academy Press.

Brookover, W., & Lezotte, L. (1979). *Changes in school characteristics coincident with changes in student achievement.* East Lansing: Michigan State University Press.

Brophy, J., & Good, T. (1986). Teacher behavior and student achievement. In M. Wittrock (Ed.), *Handbook of research on teaching* (pp. 340–370). New York: Macmillan.

Bryk, A., Lee, V., & Holland, P. (1993). *Catholic schools and the common good.* Cambridge, MA: Harvard University Press.

Bryk, A. S., & Driscoll, M. E. (1988). *The high school as community: Contextual influences, and consequences for students and teachers.* Madison: University of Wisconsin–Madison, National Center on Effective Secondary Schools.

Bryk, A. S., & Schneider, B. (2002). *Trust in schools: A core resource for improvement.* New York: Russell Sage Foundation.

Bryk, A. S., Sebring, P. B., Kerbow, D., Rollow, S., & Easton, J. Q. (1999). *Charting Chicago school reform: Democratic localism as a lever for change.* Boulder, CO: Westview Press.

Bryk, A. S., Thum, Y. M., Eaton, J. Q., & Luppescu, S. (1998). *Academic productivity of Chicago public elementary schools.* Chicago: Consortium on Chicago School Research.

Cavalluzzo, L., Lopez, D., Ross, J., Larson, M., with Miguel, M. (2005). *A Study of the Effectiveness and Cost of AEL's Online Professional Development Program in Reading in Tennessee.* Retrieved 2005, from http://www.ael.org. Copyright © 2005, Edvantia. Reprinted with permission.

Center for Data-Driven Reform in Education.

Chadwick, K. (2004). *Improving schools through community engagement: A practical guide for educators.* Thousand Oaks, CA: Corwin Press.

Charney, R. S. (1992). *Teaching children to care: Management in the responsive classroom.* Greenfield, MA: Northeast Foundation for Children.

Charney, R. S., & Wood, R. (1981). *The responsive classroom approach to instruction.* Greenfield, MA: Northeast Foundation for Children.

Chrispeels, J. H., Brown, J. H., & Castillo, S. (2000). School leadership teams: Factors that influence their development and effectiveness. *Advances in Research and Theories of School Management and Educational Policy, 4,* 39–73.

Chubb, J. E., & Moe, T. M. (1990). *Politics, markets, and America's schools.* Washington, DC: Brookings Institution.

Clark, D. L., Lotto, L. S., & McCarthy, M. (1980). *Why do some urban schools succeed?* Bloomington, IN: Phi Delta Kappa.

Clune, W. (1998). *Toward a theory of systemic reform: The case of nine NSF statewide systemic initiatives.* Madison: University of Wisconsin–Madison, Wisconsin Center for Education Research.

Coggshall, J. (2004). Reform refractions: Organizational perspectives on standards-based reform. In W. K. Hoy & C. G. Miskel (Eds.), *Educational administration, policy and reform* (pp. 1–24). Greenwich, CT: Information Age Publishing.

Cohen, D. K., & Hill, H. C. (2000). Instructional policy and classroom performance: The mathematics reform in California. *Teachers College Record, 102*(2), 294–343.

Coleman, J. S., Campbell, E., Hobson, C., McPartland, J., Mood, A., Weinfield, F., et al. (1966). *Equality of educational opportunity.* Washington, DC: U.S. Government Printing Office.

Coleman, J. S., & Hoffer, T. (1987). *Public and private high schools: The impact of the community.* New York: Basic Books.

Comer, J. (1980). *School power.* New York: Free Press.

Copeland, M. (2003). Leadership of inquiry: Building and sustaining capacity for school improvement. *Educational Evaluation and Policy Analysis, 25,* 375–395.

Council of Chief State School Officers. (2005). *Surveys of enacted curriculum: Tools and services to assist educators.* Washington, DC: Author.

Crone, D. A., & Horner, R. H. (2003). *Building positive behavior support systems in schools.* New York: Guilford Press.

D'Agostino, J. V., Borman, G. D., Hedges, L. V., & Wong, K. K. (1998). Longitudinal achievement and Chapter I coordination in high-poverty schools: A multi-level analysis of the prospects data. *Journal of Education for Students Placed at Risk, 3*(4), 401–420.

Darling-Hammond, L. (1997). *The right to learn: A blueprint for creating schools that work.* San Francisco: Jossey-Bass.

Darling-Hammond, L. (2000). *Solving the dilemmas of teacher supply, demand, and standards: How we can ensure a competent, caring, and qualified teacher for every child.* New York: National Commission on Teaching and America's Future.

Darling-Hammond, L., & Snyder, J. (2000). Authentic assessment of teaching in context. *Teaching and Teacher Education, 16,* 523–545.

Darling-Hammond, L., Wise, A., & Klein, S. (1998). *A license to teach: Building a profession for 21st century schools.* San Francisco: Jossey-Bass.

Davis, D., Ellet, C., & Annunziata, J. (2003). Teacher evaluation, leadership and learning organizations. *Journal of Personnel Evaluation and Education, 16*(4), 287–301.

Desimone, L., Garet, M., Birman, B., Porter, A., & Yoon, K. (2002). How do district management and implementation strategies relate to the quality of the professional development that districts provide to teachers? *Teachers College Record, 104*(7), 1265–1312.

Desimone, L., Porter, A., Birman, B., Garet, M., Yoon, K. (2005). Keying in to high quality professional development: District strategies and professional development features that contribute to quality programs. *The Newsletter of the Comprehensive Center-Region VI, 8*(1), 3–7.

Desimone, L., Porter, A., Garet, M., Yoon, K., & Birman, B. (2002). Effects of professional development on teachers' instruction: Results from a three-year study. *Educational Evaluation and Policy Analysis, 24*(2), 81–112.

Dixon, N. (1999). *The organization learning cycle: How we can learn collectively.* London: Gower.

Dreeben, R. (1994). The sociology of education: Its development in the Unites States. In A. Pallas (Ed.), *Research in sociology of education and socialization* (Vol. 10, pp. 7–52). Greenwich, CT: JAI Press.

Edmonds, R. R. (1979). Effective schools for the urban poor. *Educational Leadership, 37,* 15–27.

Education Sciences Reform Act of 2002. Retrieved December 2007 from http://www.ed.gov/policy/rschstat/leg/PL107-279.pdf

Elliott, S. N. (1993). *Caring to learn: A report on the positive impact of a social curriculum.* Greenfield, MA: Northeast Foundation for Children.

Elliott, S. N. (1997). *The Kensington responsive classroom study.* Greenfield, MA: Northeast Foundation for Children.

Epstein, J. L. (1992). *School and family partnerships.* Report No. 6. Baltimore: Johns Hopkins University.

Epstein, J., & Sanders, M. (2006). Prospects for change: Preparing educators for school, family, and community partnerships. *Peabody Journal of Education, 81*(2), 81–120.

Epstein, J. L., Sanders, M. G., Simon, B. S., Salinas, K. C., Jansorn, N. R., & Van Voorhis, F. L. (2002). *School, family, and community partnerships: Your handbook for action* (2nd ed.). Thousand Oaks, CA: Corwin Press.

Epstein, J., Simon, B., & Salinas, K. (1997). *Involving parents in homework in the middle grades* (Phi Delta Kappa Research Bulletin No. 18). Bloomington, IN: Phi Delta Kappa.

Epstein, J. L. (1995). School/family/community partnerships: Caring for the children we share. *Phi Delta Kappan, 76,* 701–712.

Epstein, J. L. (2001). *School, family, and community partnerships: Preparing educators and improving schools.* Boulder, CO: Westview Press.

Epstein, J. L., & Sheldon, S. B. (2002). Present and accounted for: Improving student attendance through family and community involvement. *Journal of Educational Research, 95*(5), 308–318.

Falk, B. (2002). Standards-based reforms: Problems and possibilities. *Phi Delta Kappa, 83*(8), 612.

Famer, E., & Taylor, R. G., (1997). *Notes on the process of benchmarking. Education, 118*(2), 317–319.

Feldman, J., & Tung, R. (2001). Using data-based inquiry and decision-making to improving instruction. *ERS Spectrum, 19*(3), 10–19.

Feuer, M., Towne, L., & Shavelson, R. (2002). Scientific culture and educational research. *Educational Researcher, 31,* 4–14.

Fuchs, L. S., Deno, S. L., & Mirkin, P. (1984). The effects of frequent curriculum-based measurement and evaluation on pedagogy, student achievement and student awareness of learning. *American Educational Research Journal, 21,* 449–460.

Fuchs, L. S., & Fuchs, D. (n.d.). *What is scientifically-based research on progress monitoring.* Retrieved January 10, 2007, from http://www.studentprogress .org/library/articles.asp#whatisresearch

Fuchs, L. S., Fuchs, D., & Courey, S. J. (2005). Curriculum-based measurement of mathematics competence: From computation to concepts and applications to real-life problem-solving. *Assessment for Effective Instruction, 30*(2), 33–46.

Fuhrman, S. H., & Elmore, R. F. (Eds.). (2004). *Redesigning accountability systems for education.* San Francisco: Jossey-Bass.

Fullan, M. (1999). *Change forces: The sequel.* Philadelphia: Falmer Press.

Gallagher, D., Bagin, D., & Moore, E. (2005). *The school and community relations.* Boston: Allyn & Bacon.

Gamoran, A. (2004). Classroom organization and instructional equity. In M. C. Wang & H. J. Walberg (Eds.), *Can unlike students learn together? Grade retention, tracking, and grouping* (pp. 141–155). Greenwich, CT: Information Age Publishing.

Gamoran, A., Anderson, C. W., Quiroz, P. A., Secada, W. G., Williams, T., & Ashmann, S. (2003). *Transforming teaching in math and science: How schools and districts can support change.* New York: Teachers College Press.

Gamoran, A., Nystrand, M., Berends, M., & LePore, P. (1995). An organizational analysis of the effects of ability grouping. *American Educational Research Journal, 32*(4), 687–715.

Gamoran, A., Porter, A. C., Smithson, J., & White, P. A. (1997). Upgrading high school mathematics instruction: Improving learning opportunities for low-achieving, low-income youth. *Educational Evaluation and Policy Analysis, 19*(4), 325–338.

Garcia-Reid, P., Reid, R., & Peterson, N. (2005). School engagement among Latino youth in an urban middle school context: Valuing the role of social support. *Education and Urban Society, 37*(3), 257–275.

Garet, M., Porter, A., Desimone, L., Birman, B., & Yoon, K. (2001). What makes professional development effective? Analysis of a national sample of teachers. *American Education Research Journal, 38*(3), 915–945.

Glennan, T. K., Bodilly, S., Galegher, J., & Kerr, K. A. (2004). *Expanding the reach of education reforms: Perspectives from leaders in the scale-up of educational interventions.* Santa Monica, CA: RAND.

Goldring, E., Porter, A., Murphy, J., Elliot, S., & Cravens, X. (2007). *Assessing learning-centered leadership: Connections to research, standards and practice.* Nashville, TN: Learning Sciences Institute and Wallace Foundation.

Goldring, E., & Sullivan, A. (1996). Beyond the boundaries: Principals, parents and communities shaping the school environment. In K. A. Leithwood, J. Chapman, P. Corson, & P. Hallinger (Eds.), *The international handbook of educational leadership and administration* (pp. 195–222). London: Kluwer.

Golds, E., Rhodes, A., Brown, S., Lytle, S., & Waff, D. (2001). *Clients, consumers, or collaborators? Parents and their roles in school reform during children achieving.* Philadelphia: Pew Charitable Trusts.

Gresham, E. M., Sugai, G., Horner, R. H., Quinn, M. M., & McInerney, M. (1998). *Classroom and school-wide practices that support student's social competence: A synthesis of research.* Washington, DC: Office of Special Education Programs.

Grissmer, D. W., Kirby, S. N., Berends, M., & Williamson, S. (1994). *Student achievement and the changing American family.* Santa Monica, CA: RAND.

Guskey, T. (2003a). How classroom assessments improving learning. *Educational Leadership, 60*(5), 6–11.

Guskey, T. (2003b). Professional development that works: What makes professional development effective? *Phi Delta Kappan, 84*(10), 748–750.

Hallinan, M., Gamoran, A., Kubitschek, W., & Loveless, T. (2003). *Stability and change in American education: Structure, process, and outcomes.* New York: Eliot Werner Publications, Inc.

Hallinger, P., & Heck, R. (2002). What do you call people with visions? The role of vision, mission, and goals in school improvement. In K. Leithwood, P. Hallinger, G. Furman, J. MacBeath, B. Mulford, & K. Riley (Eds.), *The second international handbook of educational leadership and administration.* Dordrecht, The Netherlands: Kluwer.

Hamilton, L. S., Stecher, B. M., & Klein, S. P. (Eds.). (2002). *Making sense of test-based accountability in education.* Santa Monica, CA: RAND.

Hargreaves, A. (1994). *Changing teachers, changing times: Teachers' work and culture in the postmodern age.* New York: Teachers College Press.

Hawley, W. D. (Ed.). (2002). *The keys to effective schools: Educational reform as continuous improvement.* Thousand Oaks, CA: Corwin Press.

Hawley, W. D., & Sykes, G. (2007). Continuous school improvement. In W. D. Hawley & D. Rollie (Eds.), *The keys to effective schools: Educational reform as continuous improvement* (pp. 153–172). Thousand Oaks, CA: Corwin Press.

Hawley, W. D., & Valli, L. (2007). Design principles for learner-centered professional development. In W. D. Hawley & D. Rollie (Eds.), *The keys to effective schools: Educational reform as continuous improvement* (pp. 117–138). Thousand Oaks, CA: Corwin Press.

Henderson, A. T., & Mapp, K. L. (2002). *A new wave of evidence: The impact of school, family, and community connections on student achievement.* Austin, TX: Southwest Educational Development Laboratory.

Henig, J. R. (1999). School choice outcomes. In S. D. Sugarman & F. R. Kemerer (Eds.), *School choice and social controversy: Politics, policy, and law* (pp. 68–110). Washington, DC: Brookings Institution.

Heubert, J. P., & Hauser, R. M. (Eds.). (1999). *High stakes testing for tracking, promotion, and graduation.* Washington, DC: National Academy Press.

Hindman, J., Brown, W., & Rogers, C. (2005). *Beyond the school: Getting the community members involved.* www.eric.ed.gov. EJ767129

Hirschman, A. O. (1970). *Exit, voice and loyalty.* Cambridge, MA: Harvard University Press.

Holcomb, E. (2002). *Getting excited about data: How to combine people, passion, and proof.* Thousand Oaks, CA: Corwin Press.

Honig, M., Kahne, J., & McLaughlin, M. (2001). School-community connections: Strengthening opportunity to learn and opportunity to teach. In V. Richardson (Ed.), *Handbook of research on teaching* (4th ed., pp. 998–1028). Washington, DC: American Educational Research Association.

Hoover-Dempsey, K., & Sandler, H. (1997). Why do parents become involved in their children's education. *Review of Educational Research, 67*(1), 3–42.

Hoy, W., & Tarter, C. J. (2004). *Administrators solving the problems of practice.* Boston: Pearson.

Ingram, D., Louis, K. S., & Schroeder, R. G. (2004). Accountability policies and teacher decision-making: Barriers to the use of data to improve practice. *Teachers College Record, 106,* 1258–1287.

Institute of Education Sciences. www.ed.ies.gov

Jacobs, B., & Ludwig, L. (2005). *Can the federal government improve education? Brookings Papers on Education Policy, 1,* 47–87.

Jandris, T. (2001). *Data-based decision-making: Essentials for principals.* Alexandria, VA: National Association of Elementary School Principals. Retrieved March 29, 2005, from http://www.eric.ed.gov

Jones, T. G. (2003). Contribution of Hispanic parents' perspectives to teacher preparation. *The School Community Journal, 13*(2), 73–97.

Juran, J. (1992). *Juran on quality by design.* New York: Free Press.

Karabel, J., & Halsey, A. H. (Eds.). (1977). *Power and ideology in education.* New York: Oxford University Press.

Kennedy, M. M., Birman, B. F., & Demaline, R. E. (1986). *The effectiveness of Chapter I services. Second interim report for the national assessment of Chapter I.* Washington, DC: U.S. Department of Education, Office of Educational Research and Improvement.

Knapp, M., Copland, M., & Talbert, J. (2003). *Leading for learning: Reflective tools for school and district leaders.* Seattle: University of Washington, Center for the Study of Teaching and Policy.

Knapp, M. S., Shields, P. M., & Turnbull, B. J. (1992). *Academic challenge for the children of poverty* (Summary report). Washington, DC: U.S. Department of Education.

Koretz, D. (2002). Limitations in the use of achievement tests as measures of educators' productivity. In E. Hanushek, J. Heckman, & D. Neal (Eds.), Designing incentives to promote human capital [Special issue]. *Journal of Human Resources, 37*(4), 752–777.

Lagermann, E. (1997). Contested terrain: A history of education research in the United States, 1890–1990. *Educational Researcher, 26*(9), 5–17.

Lareau, A., & Horvat, E. M. (1999). Moments of social inclusion and exclusion: Race, class, and cultural capital in family-school relationships. *Sociology of Education, 72*(1), 37–53. 0423.

Larson, M. (2005). *Professional development models: A review of the literature.* Retrieved January 2005 from http://www.ael.org

Learning First Alliance. (2005). Practical guide to promoting America's public schools. Retrieved February 2005 from www.learningfirst.org Learning Points Associates. (n.d.) *The building blocks initiative for standards-based reform artifact.* Retrieved February 2005 from http://www.centerforcsri.org/pubs/reallocation/analysisforms.html

Lee, V. E., Smith, J. B., & Croninger, R. G. (1995). *Another look at high school restructuring: More evidence that it improves student achievement and more insights into why.* Madison, WI: Center on Organization and Restructuring of Schools.

Levesque, K., Bradby, D., Rossi, K., Teitelbaum, P. (1998). *At your fingertips: Using everyday data to improve schools.* Berkeley: MPR Associates.

Linn, R. L. (2000). Assessment and accountability. *Educational Researcher, 29*(2), 4–16.

Linn, R. L., Baker, E. L., & Betebenner, D. (2002). Accountability systems: Implications of requirements of the No Child Left Behind Act of 2001. *Educational Researcher, 31*(6), 3–16.

Little, J. W. (2002). Professional communication and collaboration. In W. D. Hawley (Ed.), *The keys to effective schools: Educational reform as continuous improvement* (pp. 43–55). Thousand Oaks, CA: Corwin Press.

Louis, K. S., Marks, H., & Kruse, S. (1996). Teachers' professional community in restructuring schools. *American Educational Research Journal, 33*(4), 75–98.

Louis, K. S., & Miles, M. B. (1990). *Improving the urban high school: What works and why.* New York: Teachers College Press.

Masden, A. S. (1994). Resilience in individual development: Successful adaptation despite risk and adversity. In M. C. Wang & E. W. Gordon (Eds.), *Educational resilience in inner-city America: Challenges and prospects* (pp. 3–26). Hillsdale, NJ: Lawrence Erlbaum Associates.

Massell, D. (1998). *State strategies for building local capacity: Addressing the needs of standards-based reform.* Philadelphia: University of Pennsylvania, Consortium for Policy Research in Education.

Mass Insight Education & Research Institute. (2007). *Building block initiatives.* Retrieved January 2007 from http://www.massinsight.org/initiatives/buildingblocks/search.aspx

McBrien, J., & Brandt, R. (1997). *The language of learning: A guide to education terms.* Alexandria, VA: Association for Supervision and Curriculum Development.

McGeehee, J., & Griffith, L. (2001). Large-scale assessments combined with curriculum alignment: Agents of change. *Theory Into Practice, 40*(2), 137.

McLaughlin, M. W., & Talbert, J. E. (2001). *Professional communities and the work of high school teaching.* Chicago: University of Chicago Press.

McPherson, R. B., Crowson, R. L., Pitner, N. J. (1986). *Managing uncertainty. Administrative theory and practice in education.* Columbus, OH: Charles E. Merrill

Mediratta, K., & Fruchter, N. (2001). *Mapping the field of organizing for school improvement: A report on education organizing in Baltimore, Chicago, Los Angeles, the Mississippi Delta, New York City, Philadelphia, San Francisco, and Washington, D.C.* New York: New York University, The Institute for Education and Social Policy.

Memphis City Public Schools. Retrieved January 2007 from http://www.mcsk12.net/admin/tlapages/literacy_sec/renlearning/index.asp; http://www.mcsk12.net/admin/tlapages/literacy_sec/renlearning/documents/Assessment Master_Teacher_Manual.pdf

Moll, L., Amanti, C., Neff, D., & Gonzalez, N. (1992). Funds of knowledge for teaching: Using a qualitative approach to connect homes and classrooms. *Theory into Practice, 11*(2), 132–141.

Mortimore, P., Sammons, P., Stoll, L., Lewis, D., & Ecob, R. (1980). *School matters: The junior years.* Somerset, UK: Open Books.

Muller, C. (1993). Parent involvement and academic achievement: An analysis of family recourses available to the child. In B. Schneider & J. Coleman (Eds.), *Parents, their children and schools* (pp. 77–113). Boulder, CO: Westview Press.

Murphy, J. (1992). School effectiveness and school restructuring: Contribution to educational improvement. *School Effectiveness and School Improvement, 3*(2), 90–109.

Murphy, J. (Ed.). (2002). *The educational leadership challenge: Redefining leadership for the 21st century: 101 yearbook of the National Society of the Study of Education, Part 1.* Chicago: University of Chicago Press.

Murphy, J., Elliott, S., Goldring, E., & Porter, A. (2007). Leadership for learning: A research based model and taxonomy of behaviors. *School Leadership and Management, 27*(2), 179–201.

Murphy, J., & Hallinger, P. (1992). The principalship in an era of transformation. *Journal of Educational Administration, 30*(3), 77–88.

National Commission on Teaching and America's Future. (1996). *What matters most: Teaching for America's future.* New York: Author.

National Research Council. (1999). *Improving student learning.* Washington, DC: National Academy Press.

Newmann, F. M. (2002). Achieving high-level outcomes for all students: The meaning of staff-shared understanding and commitment. In W. D. Hawley (Ed.), *The keys to effective schools: Educational reform as continuous improvement* (pp. 28–42). Thousand Oaks, CA: Corwin Press.

Newmann, F. M., & Associates. (1996). *Authentic achievement: Restructuring school for intellectual quality.* San Francisco: Jossey-Bass.

Newmann, F. M., Smith, B.A., Allensworth, E., & Bryk, A. S. (2001). Instructional program coherence: What it is and why it should guide school improvement policy. *Educational Evaluation and Policy Analysis, 23,* 297–321.

Newmann, F. M., & Wehlage, G. H. (1995). *Successful school restructuring: A report to the public and educators by the Center on Organization and Restructuring of Schools.* Alexandria, VA: Association for Supervision and Curriculum Development; Reston, VA: National Association for Secondary School Principals.

Nichols, B. W., & Singer, K. P. (2000). Professional development that addresses school capacity: Lessons from urban elementary schools. *American Journal of Education, 108,* 259–299.

Oakes, J., Gamoran, A., & Page, R. (1992). Curriculum differentiation: Opportunities, outcomes, and meaning. In P. W. Jackson (Ed.), *Handbook of research on curriculum* (pp. 570–608). Washington, DC: American Educational Research Association.

Paulson, L. F., Paulson, P. R., & Meyer, C. (1991). What makes a portfolio a portfolio? *Educational Leadership, 48,* 60–63.

Popham, W. J. (2006). *Assessment for Educational Leaders.* Boston: Pearson.

Porter, A. (2003). An emerging consensus. *Phi Delta Kappan, 85*(3), 247–249.

Porter, A. C. (1994). National standards and school improvement in the 1990s: Issues and promise. *American Journal of Education, 102*(4), 421–449.

Porter, A. C. (2002). Measuring the content of instruction: Uses in research and practice. *Educational Researcher, 31*(7), 3–14.

Porter, A. C., Garet, M., Desimone, L., Birman, B., & Yoon, K. (2003). Providing effective professional development: Lessons from the Eisenhower program. *Science Educator, 12*(1), 23–40.

Pounder, D., Reitzug, U., & Young, M. (2002). Preparing school leaders for school improvement, social justice, and community. In J. Murphy (Ed.), *The educational leadership challenge: Redefining leadership for the 21st century* (pp. 261–288). Chicago: University of Chicago Press.

Powell, T. (1995). Total quality management as competitive advantage: A review and empirical study. *Strategic Management Journal, 16*(10), 15–37.

Purkey, S. C., & Smith, M. S. (1983). Effective schools: A review. *The Elementary School Journal, 83*(4), 426–452.

Rothman, R., Slattery, J. B., Vranek, J. L., & Resnick, L. B. (2002). *Benchmarking and alignment of standards and testing* (CSE Technical Report No. 566).

Los Angeles: University of California, National Center for Research on Evaluation, Standards, and Student Testing.

Rothstein, R. (1998). *The way we were? The myths and realities of America's student achievement.* New York: Century Foundation Press.

Rutter, M., Maughan, B., Mortimore, P., Ouston, J., & Smith, A. (1979). *Fifteen thousand hours: Secondary schools and their effects on children.* Cambridge, MA: Harvard University Press.

Sanders, M. (2001). A study of the role of community in comprehensive school, family and community partnership programs. *Elementary School Journal, 102*(1), 19–34.

Sanders, M. (2006). *Building school-community partnerships: Collaboration for student success.* Thousand Oaks, CA: Corwin Press.

Sanders, M. G., & Harvey, A. (2000, April). *Developing comprehensive programs of school, family, and community partnerships: The community perspective.* Paper presented at the Meeting of the American Educational Research Association, New Orleans, LA.

Schmidt, W. H., McKnight, C. C., Houang, R. T., Wang, H., Wiley, D. E., Cogan, L. S., et al. (2001). *Why schools matter: A cross-national comparison of curriculum and learning.* San Francisco: Jossey-Bass.

Schmidt, W. H., McKnight, C. C., & Raizen, S. A. (1997). *A splintered vision: An investigation of U.S. science and mathematics* (Executive summary). Lansing, MI: Michigan State University, U.S. National Research Center for the Third International Mathematics and Science Study. Retrieved December 1, 1999, from http://ustimss.msu.edu/splintrd.pdf

Scribner, J. D., Young, M. D., & Pedroza, A. (1999). Building collaborative relationships with parents. In P. Reyes, J. D. Scribner, & A. Paredes-Scribner (Eds.), *Lessons from high-performing Hispanic schools: Creating learning communities* (pp. 36–60). New York: Teachers College Press.

Sebring, P. B., & Bryk, A. (2000). School leadership and the bottom line in Chicago. *Phi Delta Kappan, 8*(6), 440–443.

Sharkey, N., & Murane, R. (2006). Tough choices in designing a formative assessment system. *American Journal of Education, 112*, 572–588.

Shaver, A. V., & Wells, R. T. (1998). Effect of Title I parent involvement on student reading and mathematics achievement. *Journal of Research and Development in Education, 31*(2), 90–97.

Sheldon, S. B. (2003). Linking school-family-community partnerships in urban elementary schools to student achievement on state tests. *Urban Review, 35*, 149–165.

Sheldon, S. B., & Epstein, J. L. (2002). Improving student behavior and discipline with family and community involvement. *Education in Urban Society, 35*(1), 4–26.

Shinn, M. R. (2002). Best practices in using curriculum-based measurement in a problem-solving model. In A. Thomas & J. Grines (Eds.), *Best practices in school psychology IV* (pp. 671–697). Bethesda, MD: National Association of School Psychologists.

Shulman, L. (2005). Seek simplicity . . . and distrust it. *Education Week, 24*(39), 36, 48.

Smith, M. S., & O'Day, J. (1991). Systemic school reform. In S. H. Fuhrman & B. Malen (Eds.), *The politics of curriculum and testing: The 1990 yearbook of the Politics of Education Association* (pp. 233–267). Bristol, PA: Falmer Press.

Smrekar, C., Guthrie, J. W., Owens, D. E., & Sims, P. G. (2001). *March towards excellence: School success and minority student achievement in Department of Defense schools* (Report to the National Education Goals Panel). Nashville, TN: Peabody College Vanderbilt University, Peabody Center for Education Policy.

Snipes, J., Doolittle, F., and Herlihy, C. (2002). *Foundations for success: Case studies of how urban school systems improve student achievement.* New York: Council of the Great City Schools and MDRC.

Study of Instructional Improvement. (2001). *Project Instruments.* Ann Arbor, MI: University of Michigan, School of Education. Retrieved April 30, 2006, from http://www.sii.soe.umich.edu/

Vinovskis, M. (1996). An analysis of the concept and uses of systemic educational reform. *American Educational Research Journal, 33*(1), 53–85.

Wang, M. C., Oates, J., & Weishew, N. L. (1995). Effective school responses to student diversity in inner-city schools: A coordinated approach. *Education and Urban Society, 27*(4), 484–503. EJ511143. Philadelphia: Temple University, The Mid-Atlantic Regional Educational Laboratory.]

Webb, N. L. (1997). *Criteria for alignment of expectations and assessments in mathematics and science education* (Research Monograph No. 6). Madison: University of Wisconsin–Madison, National Institute for Science Education.

Wehlage, G., Newmann, F., & Secada, W. (1996). Standards of authentic achievement and pedagogy. In F. Newmann & Assoc. (Eds.), *Authentic achievement: Restructuring schools for intellectual quality* (pp. 21–48). San Francisco: Jossey-Bass.

Westat and Policy Studies Associates. (2001). *The longitudinal evaluation of change and performance in Title I schools.* Washington, DC: U.S. Department of Education, Office of the Deputy Secretary, Planning and Evaluation Service.

What Works Clearing House, U.S. Department of Education. (2007a). *Identifying and implementing educational practices supported by rigorous evidence: A user friendly guide.* Retrieved January 2007 from http://www.ed.gov/rschstat/research/pubs/rigorousevid/index.html

What Works Clearinghouse, U.S. Department of Education. (2007b). WWC intervention report: *Elementary school math.* Retrieved January 2007 from http://ies.ed.gov/ncee/wwc/reports/elementary_math/sesm/index.asp

What Works Clearinghouse, U.S. Department of Education. (2007c). WWC intervention report: *Everyday mathematics.* Retrieved January 2007 from http://ies.ed.gov/ncee/wwc/reports/elementary_math/eday_math/

Whitehurst, G. J. (2002, June 25). Statement of Grover J. Whitehurst, Assistant Secretary for Research and Improvement, before the Senate Committee on Health, Education, Labor and Pensions. Washington, DC: U.S. Department of Education. Retrieved January 2007 from http://www.ed.gov/news/speeches/2002/06/06252002.html

Wong, K. K., Hedges, L. V., Borman, G. D., & D'Agostino, J. V. (1996). *Prospectus: Special analyses* (Final report). Washington, DC: U.S. Department of Education.

Wyman, J. C. (2005). Involving teachers in data-driven decision-making: Using computer data systems to support teacher inquiry and reflection. *Journal of Education for Students Placed at Risk, 10*(3), 295–308.

Zangwill, W. I., & Kantor, P. B. (1998). Towards a theory of continuous improvement and the learning curve. *Management Science, 44*(7), 910–920.

Index

Hawaii

CORWIN PRESS

The Corwin Press logo—a raven striding across an open book—represents the union of courage and learning. Corwin Press is committed to improving education for all learners by publishing books and other professional development resources for those serving the field of PreK–12 education. By providing practical, hands-on materials, Corwin Press continues to carry out the promise of its motto: **"Helping Educators Do Their Work Better."**

The American Association of School Administrators, founded in 1865, is the professional organization for more than 13,000 educational leaders across the United States. AASA's mission is to support and develop effective school system leaders who are dedicated to the highest quality public education for all children. For more information, visit www.aasa.org.